Building A CITY ON A HILL

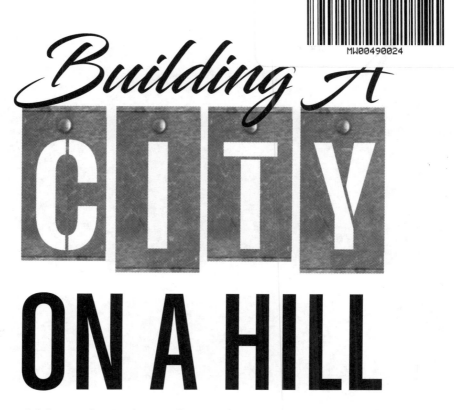

African American Communities of Purpose

Written and Edited by Carey Latimore, Ph.D.

UMI (Urban Ministries, Inc.)
P. O. Box 436987
Chicago, Illinois 60643-6987
1-800-860-8642
www.urbanministries.com

First Edition

First Printing

Scripture quotations marked KJV, or unmarked, are from King James Version.

Scripture quotations marked NIV are taken from the HOLY BIBLE, NEW INTERNATIONAL VERSION®, copyright© 1973, 1978, 1984, 2011. Used by permission of Zondervan. All rights reserved.

Scripture quotations marked NASB are taken from the NEW AMERICAN STANDARD BIBLE®, COPYRIGHT© 1960, 1962, 1963, 1971, 1972, 1973, 1975, 1977, 1995 by The Lockman Foundation. Used by permission.

Library of Congress Cataloguing in Publications Data

Building A City On A Hill: African American Communities of Purpose Student Book
ISBN-13: 978-1-68353-127-2

Printed in the United States of America.

Acknowledgments

I believe this project is divinely inspired. It began when Lakita Wright from Urban Ministries, Inc. contacted me. Because I was out of the country and didn't have a reliable wi-fi signal, it took me some time to respond. About three weeks later, after I returned to the United States, I visited UMI headquarters in Calumet City, Illinois. While there, Lakita and Jeffrey Wright pitched the idea for me to write a book on Black communities that would be part of their adult VBS 2018 curriculum. I wanted to be part of this project. During my short time there I had the honor to speak with Dr. Melvin Banks, the man who started all of this. In many ways, I now believe that UMI reflects the spirit of the communities in this book. My experiences at the headquarters and throughout the duration of this project have renewed my commitment to my field and to my community. I want to thank the entire team at UMI, particularly Chris O'Neal and Ramon Mayo, who have worked diligently with me to get this project completed on time.

I also want to acknowledge my family. Indeed, I am blessed with such a great family. My amazing wife, Almie, my rock, has been such a tremendous support throughout this project and everything else. I can't thank her enough for her devotion to me. My parents and siblings have lived lives that demonstrate the value of belief and hard work and I will always be indebted to them. I also thank my Pastor, Otis Mitchell, and the Mount Zion First Baptist Church of San Antonio, Texas, for all of their love and support.

I want to express my sincere gratitude and appreciation to Nina Nevill, my research assistant, who has provided tremendous assistance to me throughout this entire process. She has been amazingly diligent and so committed to this project.

Finally, I must both acknowledge and thank my Lord and Savior Jesus Christ for His love, grace, and mercy.

Table of Contents

Introduction

Growing up in a small rural community in Virginia's tidewater has helped me understand the strong connections faith and family have to community identity and investment. As a people, we invest in the things we value and treasure. My great-great grandmother acquired the first piece of our family farm shortly after Reconstruction's end. Her son, my great grandfather, purchased more land and farmed it during the early twentieth century.

My grandparents continued farming this land until their deaths. On that same land, my father established a fiberglass boat repair business. In the same county of my youth, my mother established a teaching career in schools still in the midst of Jim Crow. My family is committed to the community and has invested in it for 140 years.

During that time, Antioch Baptist has remained the center of my family's lives. It is a small yet beautiful Baptist church located roughly a mile away from our family farm. As it is in many rural churches, services are not held every Sunday. Instead, we attended service on first and third Sundays. The pastor, as it has been for the last century, also led our sister church that held service on second and forth Sundays. On the fifth Sunday, all the local Black Baptist churches came together for literary union.

Even now, I smile when I think about all the lessons I learned on Sunday mornings from Sunday School to the main service. There was a wholeness in the church and its congregants. The church compound also included the old church school and the church graveyard. My father and ancestors attended that old, one-room-church school. The old graveyard is the resting place of my grandparents, great-grandparents, and probably my great-great grandmother.

I am now 42 years old and my community has experienced so many changes over time. But the one constant is that my community thrived when families and friends invested in young people. This is what happened in my life and the lives of the individuals in the community where I grew up. Most of us no longer live there, but many of us maintain a strong connection to it. We may not be rich in material things, but many of us have retained a fire for the Lord, a desire to serve our communities, and a push to own a home and the land underneath it.

I believe it is important for African Americans, at this crucial period in American history, to take an assessment of where our communities stand. Today, it seems as if many of our communities and institutions are in crisis.

One of the reasons is a lack of investment. Many of us have looked outward for resources to help our community neglecting the power of faith and self-determination. People without hope do not believe they have the ability to effect change.

The community builders detailed in the pages of this book exhibited bold devotion to their communities. No matter the obstacles, the men and women in this book left us a road map for community renewal and redemption. They stepped out, created, and fought to attain "Canaan" under tremendous pressures.

The communities in this book, from Mound Bayou to Freedmen's Town, are but ten examples of the type of building that can strengthen our nation's communities. I hope that after reading this book, you will not only read more about the communities introduced, but you will become more active in your communities and help them experience revival.

I leave you with a call to action. A few of the communities explored in this book are in rural America. This was by design. Most of our ancestors came from these places and there was a time when Black farmers made up a significant number of American farmers. Today, there are very few Black farmers left in our nation. There was a time when African Americans owned substantial acres. Today, it is depressing to think of how much land our community has lost.

While we have given significant attention to urban gentrification, there is a similar phenomenon of rural gentrification happening right before our eyes. As a community, we have been too silent about this and even contributed to this destruction of our rural communities, churches, and settlements. The time has come for us to reverse this trend and reclaim our legacies to leave tangible resources to the next generation.

Carey Latimore IV
San Antonio, Texas

MOUND BAYOU
BUILD ON JESUS

Then David the king stood up upon his feet, and said, Hear me, my brethren, and my people: As for me, I had in mine heart to build an house of rest for the ark of the covenant of the LORD, and for the footstool of our God, and had made ready for the building. (1 Chronicles 28:2 KJV)

American racism has created very specific challenges for Black families that, over time, have led to an erosion of the nuclear family structure. Although two-parent households aren't always possible, strong nuclear households have historically provided both economic and social benefits to our communities.[1] Strong and stable families provide self-esteem and moral grounding to the successive generations.

Even though some researchers have argued that slavery destroyed the Black family, the research clearly shows that Black men and women were initially successful in establishing stable family networks both during and after slavery. By the first decade of the twentieth century, very little distinguished Black and White families in their makeup. The legacy of slavery and racism, however, did lead to one distinction: To negotiate the lines between Black and White, Black people had to develop closer ties with extended family, both by blood and by adopted kin. These types of relationships led to networks of mutual aid collaboration. Whether it was through business, family, fraternal, religious, or social relationships, these connections created a buffer against racial isolation. Although racism presented many challenges to Black people, it meant that Black people had to collaborate amongst

---

[1] Dalton Garis, "Poverty, Single-Parent Households, and Youth At-Risk Behavior: An Empirical Study," *Journal of Economic Issues*, Vol 32 (Dec. 1998): 1079-1105.

themselves to establish strong, stable, and sustainable communities. The story of Mound Bayou, one of the first incorporated Black towns in the United States, is a prime example of how Black families and communities can work together to establish long-lasting legacies.[2]

Parents establishing a legacy for their children

The Bible speaks to parents leaving legacies to their children. In Proverbs 13:22, the writer speaks of a "good man leaving an inheritance to his children's children." This speaks to the long-term vision that we need to have, not just for ourselves, but for those who will come after us. This long-term planning is clearly evident in the building of the temple. In II Samuel 7:1-17, David wanted to build God's house. He regretted sitting in a beautiful palace while God was worshiped in a tent. This bothered him so much that he set his mind to building a temple in Jersualem. David never saw the temple constructed. The prophet, Nathan, let him know that God would not allow him to build the house. Instead, his son, Solomon, would build the house. David listened to God, but at the same time, he prepared materials and plans for Solomon to construct the temple. This is very similar to the relationship between Benjamin T. Montgomery and Isaiah Montgomery, one of the founders of Mound Bayou.

Although Isaiah Montgomery was one of the founders of Mound Bayou, it was his father, Benjamin T. Montgomery, who originally dreamed of establishing a Black town. Born in 1819 in Virginia, as a young man, Benjamin T. Montgomery was sold to Joseph Davis, the younger brother of future Confederate President Jefferson Davis. Forced to move to Mississippi, Isaiah Montgomery escaped captivity after being sold to Davis. Eventually captured, he defended his status to Davis until they "reached a mutual understanding and established a mutual confidence time only served to strengthen throughout their long and eventful

---

[2] Daniel Patrick Moynihan, *The Negro Family: The case for national action. Office of policy planning and research.* United States Department of labor. Washington: Government printing Office, 1965; John McWhorter, "Were There Really Fewer Two-Parent Black Families During Slavery than There Are Today?" *New Republic*, July 12, 2011. Accessed October 9, 2017, https://newrepublic.com/article/91933/slavery-Black-families-single-parents.

connection." Even though he remained enslaved, his act of defiance gained his master's respect. He secured from Davis opportunities to learn, and by the time slavery ended, he had enough skills to become a successful businessman. He knew how to farm cotton, survey land, and handle employment books. When the Davis family abandoned the plantation during the Civil War, Montgomery was left in control it.[3]

Although a privileged slave on the plantation, Montgomery seized the opportunity for freedom when it presented itself. When the Union Army came to the plantation, he and his entire family escaped with them, eventually going to Ohio. The sojourn of the Montgomery family in Ohio did not last long. Isaiah Montgomery dreamed to return to his home and establish a community of freed people. When he did return, he united with other Black leaders who wanted to own land and grow cotton on the Davis plantation. They formed a committee and requested permission to acquire the land from the Freedmen's Bureau, a government organization established to help people recover from the war. Probably as a result of racism, the bureau resisted the committee's demands. Refusing to be deterred, Montgomery turned to his former owner, Joseph Davis, who arranged to sell the entire plantation to his former slave. Montgomery agreed to pay the Davis family the entire sum over 10 years. In the 1870s, difficult economic times led to Montgomery's inability to pay the mortgage and the property reverted to the Davis family.[4]

Isaiah Montgomery learned much from his parents' successes and failures. Born in 1847, he was barely a teenager when the Civil War began. He learned how to read and write and was a clerk for the Davis family. Like his father, he wanted to establish a "colony" for African Americans where Black people could live independently. He maintained the old familial relationships from the Davis plantation and, in doing so, pooled together sparse resources. Isaiah Montgomery's first attempt to live this lifestyle came in the late 1880s when he united with other

---

[3] Janet Sharp Hermann, "Reconstruction in a Microcosm," *Journal of Negro History* vol. 65 (Autumn 1980): 316
[4] Hermann, 312-335.

former slaves from the Davis plantation to invest in land in Nicodemus, Kansas.[5] Even then, he longed to establish a colony in Mississippi.

Dreams of establishing a colony in Mississippi were helped by industrialization. During Reconstruction, southern states began to industrialize and they started to strengthen their transportation networks, a transition that opened new territories for exploration. Railroad companies wanted to make inroads into the uncultivated lands of the Mississippi Delta. These railroads needed laborers in the areas of the uncultivated land. Montgomery seized this opportunity. Together with his cousin Benjamin Green, he purchased more than 800 acres of land on the grounds where the railroad wanted to expand to. With this initial purchase, Montgomery boldly took his first steps to building a community of Black landowners. Montgomery later recalled that he told the settlers to not "fear the difficulties" in front of them. He asked them "Have you and your forefathers not for centuries braved the miasma [bad smell] and hewn down forests at the command of your master?" He told them that this was a chance to build on their families' legacies and establish a place where "they may worship and develop under their own vine and fig tree."[6]

Stacking Stones

To survive the American frontier, Mound Bayou's residents worked diligently to establish a strong foundation. Located in the northwestern part of Mississippi, a region so undeveloped it had been referred to as a "dense jungle," it had to be cleared of its forest to construct its roads. The first settlers to the area were not ordinary farmers or businessmen, but they were men and women committed to having a piece of their dreams. They also knew how to produce and sell cotton. Isaiah Montgomery recruited families from across the country,

---

[5] Thomas H. Arnold, "Ex-Slaves Dream of a Model Negro Colony Comes True," *New York Times*, Jun 12, 1910, assessed October 9, 2017, https://search-proquest-com.libproxy.trinity.edu/docview/97110143?accountid=7103; Mound Bayou Morns Slave Who Founded Negro City," *New York Times*, Apr 27, 1924, assessed October 9, 2017, https://search-proquest-com.libproxy.trinity.edu/docview/103394215?accountid=7103. ;Roy L. Brooks, *Integration or separation?: a strategy for racial equality* (Cambridge, MA: Harvard University Press, 1999), 173

[6] Arnold, *New York Times*, June 12, 1910

promising them solitude and an opportunity to have a life outside White control. Eventually, "immigrants [African Americans] from all parts of Mississippi, and a certain number from other states" came to Mound Bayou.[7]

There were many reasons African Americans moved to Mound Bayou, but escaping racism was the core reason. Life in the era of Jim Crow, was extremely difficult. Booker T. Washington, a close associate of Isaiah Montgomery, wrote that some of the settlers who came to Mound Bayou were victims of whitecapping. Whitecaps [persons involved in whitecapping] were White farmers, often from the poorer agricultural and tenant farming class, who felt compromised by Southern industrialization. They were numerous in Mississipi. The whitecaps, felt that merchants and Black farmers and tenants were conspiring to destroy their economic opportunities. They believed this would eventually push them into sharecropping and tenant farming. They led campaigns to push African Americans from the land they lived on and often resorted to violence to achieve their goals.[8] As victims of whitecapping, residents of Mound Bayou certainly feared what working alongside White farmers could mean. Indeed, Booker T. Washington argued that "it has been the constant aim of the men who founded the colony to preserve it as a distinctively Negro enterprise."[9]

Being removed from the threat of violence and protected by the town founders' amicable relationships with prominent southern White men, helped Mound Bayou thrive. It was a place where Black people purchased land and set up homesteads. Booker T. Washington estimated that by 1910 the area included more than 30,000 acres, "all owned by Negroes, most of them small farmers who till 40- and 80-acre tracts." On those lands, Black farmers could harvest cotton or grain crops. Some could be sold for profit and the other produced for their

---

[7] Booker T. Washington, "A Town Owned by Negroes: Mound Bayou, Miss., An Example of Thrift and Self-Government," *World's Work*, 14 (July, 1907): 9126

[8] William F. Holmes, "Whitecapping: Agrarian Violence in Mississippi, 1902-1906." *The Journal of Southern History* 35, vol. 2 (1969): 165-67. doi:10.2307/2205711.

[9] Washington, 9128

own use. All together, it is estimated that the entire area included about 800 families and about 4,000 people.[10]

Perhaps learning from his father's mistake with large debt, Isaiah Montgomery and other Mound Bayou leaders established an economic system centered around the homestead and economic discipline. They encouraged residents to purchase their own homes and work off the land they owned. This arrangement is in stark contrast to tenant farming and sharecropping, two of the more exploitative labor systems so many Black farmers found themselves in during the late 19th century. In both of these labor relationships, farmers did not own land and paid the owners of the land for its use. In contrast, farmers in Mound Bayou had the opportunity to purchase "his land from a member of his own race, who is interested in his success and upbuilding, at a low price and a low rate of interest rather than buying from a White man at a high price and ruinous rate of interest or renting it on a crop-sharing contract."[11]

Within twenty years, the value of Mound Bayou's land had increased greatly and residents had established a sustainable community. Residents in the town and countryside also found all their basic necessities within Mound Bayou. By 1910, more than 50 stores and shops existed in the town including several grocery stores, carpentry stores, insurance agencies, and real estate agencies. The high point of economic development in Mound Bayou occurred in January, 1904, when the town leaders organized and opened the Bank of Mound Bayou. The bank provided loans to local residents to establish their businesses. The bank also provided loans for people to fix their houses.[12]

The bank was led by the most prominent men in the community. Indeed, the close connections between residents in Mound Bayou is demonstrated by the bank leadership. John Francis was the first bank

---

[10] Washington, 9125-9126

[11] Arnold, *New York Times*, June 12, 1910

[12] Arnold, *New York Times*, June 12, 1910

president. Born in Louisiana, Francis came to Mound Bayou and set up a farm and a grocery store. Around 1898, he married Eva Green, the widow of Benjamin Green, one of the founders of Mound Bayou who was murdered in 1896. The founder of the bank, Charles Banks, a close associate of Isaiah Montgomery, was a businessman in nearby Clarksdale and moved to Mound Bayou to further his career. None of these men came from elite and privileged backgrounds. They were self-made men who wanted to help other Blacks achieve similar goals.[13]

Not long after forming the bank, the leaders of the community created the Mound Bayou Loan and Investment Company, which was a loan company that sold stock to the farmers. The intent of the company was to "take over the mortgages of those members of the community who were not able to pay the loans as they fell due, and at the same time provide a way by which the owners of the land might accumulate a sum sufficient to pay off the indebtedness for which the mortgage was issued."[14]

Unfortunately, by 1914, financial problems and a nationwide recession led to the bank's closure. Banks and Montgomery attempted to establish another bank in 1916. This bank would also fail eight years later. The pressures of economic recession and migration, particularly between 1917 and 1940, had a tremendous effect on the community. By this time a rift between Isaiah Montgomery, Charles Banks, and other community leaders sharply divided the community.[15]

The story of Mound Bayou follows a similar pattern to other Black towns and settlements in the early twentieth century. Research shows that between 1870 and 1900 African Americans significantly closed the racial gap in landownership and homeownership. However, after Black landownership peaked around 1915. There are a number of contributing factors to the decline of Black landownership. The

---

[13] Washington, 9127-29; See David H. Jackson, *A Chief Lieutenant of the Tuskegee Machine: Charles Banks of Mississippi* (Gainsville: University Press of Florida).

[14] Washington, 9128.

[15] Rachel Kranz and Ian C. Friedman, *African-American business leaders & entrepreneurs* (New York: Facts On File, 2014), 13-14.

migration out of the south that occurred in the years following World War I changed the trajectory of Black landholding. As hundreds of thousands of Blacks left the rural south for urban locations in the North as part of the Great Migration, many of them lost interest in owning rural land and home ownership.[16]

Keeping the faith

Mound Bayou was much more than an African American economic center. The settlers of Mound Bayou established numerous houses of worship. According to the website for Mound Bayou, the Montgomery family helped establish the AME church in Mound Bayou. This would explain the significant number of AME pastors living within Mound Bayou throughout the early twentieth century. The largest churches included the Green Grove Missionary Baptist Church and the Bethel African Methodist Episcopal Church. Green Grove Missionary Baptist church even had its own newspaper, *The Baptist Echo*. This was one of several newspapers produced by members of the Mound Bayou community.[17]

Religion and education worked together in Mound Bayou. In addition to the public school, there was the Mound Bayou Industrial Institute, an educational institution that provided agricultural vocational training to men and women. Another institution in Mound Bayou was the Baptist College, which in 1910 had approximately 200 students. Religious denominations also united to establish a community moral code. In the early years of settlement, alcohol and gambling were strictly prohibited. In his essay about Mound Bayou, Booker T. Washington stated that local churches worked together to ensure that all of the couples living together had to be married. He writes "some years ago, when the question was an "issue" in the community, a

---

[16] William J. Collins and Robert A. Margo, *"Race and Home Ownership: A Century-Long View,"* *Explorations in Economic History*, 37 (2001): 68-92;
Christian, Colmore, Rory Fraser, and Amadou Diop "African-American Land Loss and Sustainable Forestry in the Southeast: An Analysis of the Issues, Opportunities, and Gaps," *Journal of Extension* 51, no. 6 (December 2013), assessed October 9, 2017, https://www.joe.org/joe/2013december/a2.php

[17] Arnold, *New York Times*, June 10, 1910

committee was appointed from each of the churches to make a house to house canvass of the colony. This canvassing was done in order to determine to what extent loose family relations existed. The report of this committee showed that there were forty families in the colony where men and women were living together outside of marriage. As a result of this report, the people of the town gave notice that these forty couples would have to marry within a certain length of time or they would be prosecuted. Nearly all of them acted upon this suggestion; the others moved away."[18]

Fraternal organizations provided another anchor of the community. The region's most prestigious fraternal organization, the International Order of Twelve Knights and Daughters of Tabor, established a hospital in Mound Bayou in 1942. The hospital not only served Mound Bayou, but also the surrounding area. Indeed, it was only one of two hospitals in the Mississippi Delta, the northwest section of Mississippi, to provide care for Black people. T.R.M. Howard, a man who emerged in the 1950s as a leader not only of Black doctors, but also emerging leaders in the Mississippi Delta, was the hospital's chief surgeon.

By 1967, the hospital lost its fraternal status and was renamed the Mound Bayou Community Hospital. As the economic conditions in the Mississippi Delta deteriorated in the early 1970s, it continued to accept all people. One journalist recalled that it was "the only Black controlled hospital in Mississippi, and the only one in the dirt poor, four-county Delta area that never turns a patient away for financial reasons." Indeed, the same article in the *Washington Post* reported that the other four hospitals in the area "have consistently shifted the burden of caring for poor people, particularly Blacks, on the Mound Bayou Community Hospital and Delta Health Center."[19]

---

[18] Washington, 9129; Arnold, *New York Times*, June 10, 1910

[19] Austin Scott, Mound bayou hospital: The medical center of last resort, *The Washington Post*, August 11, 1974, assessed October 9, 2017, https://search-proquest-com.libproxy.trinity.edu/docview/146135423?account id=7103 ; Scott, *Washington Post*, 1974, Aug 11).

Will our communities rise from the dust?

The economic prospects in Mound Bayou declined in the years after World War I as depopulation and mismanagement derailed the town's progress. By 1982, the entire town was in debt. Federal funds had run dry and telephone lines from city hall were cut off. A newspaper report from 1982 stated that the city sheriff had not been paid in months. Once a place Black people went to make a living, the sheriff of the county was so poor that he could not pay $100 a month to rent a trailer.[20]

Nevertheless, the Black community in Mound Bayou laid the groundwork for economic and social uplift. Mound Bayou reveals the variety of ways God provides even in the midst of difficult storms. At the same time, the experiences of the pioneers at Mound Bayou point to the reality of renewal. Communities rise from the dust; they rededicate themselves. Benjamin Montgomery lost the Davis plantation, but his community acquired something better. Mound Bayou prospered when it focused on family, community, self-sufficiency and independence. The cooperation between residents and their desires to keep capital and investment within the community placed Mound Bayou on a profitable track.

While much interest has been placed in fighting urban gentrification and ameliorating the urban condition, we have not focused on the plight of the conditions in the rural South. Even though most African Americans have their foundations in the American South, after moving to the cities and suburbs many left their legacy behind. Much land was lost due to racially motivated use of eminent domain or other state and national codes that have often been used as a means to unjustly acquire African American land. But we have to also recognize that we have not been the best stewards of our land either.

---

[20] Art Harris, "Under Knife, Black Town Finds Itself Going Broke: Mound Bayou Going Broke, Victim of the Budget Knife," *Washington Post*, April 18, 1982, assessed Octover 9, 2017, https://search-proquest-com.libproxy.trinity.edu/docview/147477937?accountid=7103

There are still reasons to have hope. African Americans still own land, particularly in the Black belt rural areas in the Mississippi Delta. Contrary to what many think, we do have capital in our communities. The problem is that we all too often do not invest it wisely. Our institutions, in particular, have a track record of recklessly spending millions on endeavors that do not build up the community. These efforts do not have any chance to build revenue at a time when our collective capital could be invested in property that would allow those same institutions to truly grow and expand. Purchasing rural land on a location outside urban centers is a cheaper alternative to the multimillion dollar construction and upkeep costs. These projects often serve more as a bragging right than as something truly intended to effect real change in our communities.

It is important to build our communities on a solid foundation. That means having the right vision and perspective for the work that is needed. The best vision is one that benefits the whole and not just a few. This kind of perspective seeks to serve rather than to be served. When wealth and status are the only goals, we all lose. The vision of Jesus that benefits communities is one that has love and service to others at its foundation. That is how our communities can withstand the rains and the winds of the storms that life brings. This is the kind of foundation that motivates people and brings about change.

Black people are witnessing another revival. It is seen as towns like Mound Bayou and Eatonville, Florida return to prominence. Mound Bayou was saved from their debt by an African American radio station in Memphis. Currently, there are plans to restore the old hospital. After many years, it appears as if Mound Bayou will rise from the dead once more. Black Americans from across the country should want to see Mound Bayou return to prominence. Our ancestors made preparations for thriving communities, it is our responsibility to see those plans fulfilled.

SENECA VILLAGE
BUILDING ON A NEW FOUNDATION

so the Negro [in the North] is free, but he cannot share the rights, pleasures, labors, griefs, or even the tomb of him whose equal he has been declared; there is nowhere where he can meet him, neither in life nor in death.[1]

Free but not Truly Free

More than any White observer of his period, Alexis de Tocqueville understood the contradictions of African American life throughout the United States. As a French diplomat, he traveled to America in 1831, spending considerable time examining its institutions. Fascinated by what he saw in the new nation, he wrote about how race dominated the American conversation socially, economically, and politically. Being sensitive to America's racial climate, he took note of the cruel affect racism and colonialism had on African Americans. Recognizing the harsh conditions African Americans who lived in the North experienced, de Tocqueville wrote "the prejudice of race appears to be stronger in the states that have abolished slavery than in those where it still exists."[2]

Since de Tocqueville visited New York City in 1831, it's possible that he considered the lives of New York City African Americans when writing his commentary. At the time, New York City had the largest Black population in the North. If de Tocqueville wanted to experience a Black community in the North, New York City would have been the perfect

---

[1] Alexis de Tocqueville, *Democracy in America* (Translated by Henry Reeve) vol. 1 (New York: The Colonial Press, 1899), 364, https://books.google.com/books?id=xZfiBEzcPTEC&printsec=frontcover&source=gbs_ge_summary_r&cad=0#v=onepage&q&f=false

[2] ibid.,

place. It's possible that he crossed paths with the African American community in Seneca Village.

Much like Abraham in the book of Genesis the slaves who escaped to the North, and some free men and women, settled in Seneca Village. They went to a land they didn't know to live a new way of life. Their aspirations were tamed by racism, but they were determined to build a community of their own. It must have been hard for them to fathom a new way of life as free people. Making a way in a society that was hostile to them meant that they had to create a life for themselves based on their own principles of freedom and self-determination.

It's the same for Blacks in the 21st century. Even as they don't experience the same type of racism as their ancestors, these descendants of slavery still have to deal with a society that approaches them with a measure of hostility.

We must trust God in the same way Abraham did to lead us to a land that we don't know.

De Tocqueville's observations highlighted the contradictions of antebellum life for free African Americans in the North. The same region that gave birth to the abolitionist movement, also had some of the most stringent laws against African Americans. By the time free Blacks established Seneca Village, the few rights and privileges they had were under a continuous assault. Not only did they see their voting privileges severely restricted, they also had to fear White and Black catchers who kidnapped Blacks and sold them into slavery. Prominent free Blacks were on guard against attacks on their businesses and community organizations.

Northern Whites felt threatened when free Blacks prospered socially and economically. This is what made a community like Seneca Village so important.

Even though it was just three miles away from the city, it was a sanctuary for free African Americans. The distance provided a buffer from the most difficult conditions within city lines. Seneca Village also presented an opportunity to own land, build new churches, operate their businesses, and educate their children with fewer distractions than in the city. By investing their time, talents, and money in Seneca Village, African Americans adopted a vision of self-determination that set them on a pathway toward agency.[3]

New York City: The Hub of Black Life

New York always has had a conflicting perspective when it came to African Americans. New York City was home to the New York Abolitionist Society, one of the most influential anti-slavery organizations in late eighteenth and early nineteenth centuries. The organization established schools in the city for Blacks and tried to influence the state legislature to end slavery. Nevertheless this organization was unable to get New York to adopt an abolition plan until 1799, making it one of the last Northern states to outlaw slavery. Moreover, the proposal adopted by the state legislature only emancipated slaves born after July 4th that year.

In 1817, the state legislature passed another law that emancipated those slaves the previous law didn't manumit, but this law only did so when they reached twenty-one years of age. Gradual abolition did not immediately free every slave, but it did contribute to a dramatic increase in the state's free African American population during the first few decades of the nineteenth century, particularly in New York City. Most free African Americans in New York City lived and congregated near Five Points, an area in southern Manhattan. A mixed neighborhood of immigrants, poor Whites, and African Americans, Five Points was one of the poorest urban communities in America. But among the tenements and overall impoverished conditions rose a number of churches and community organizations.

---

[3] Shane White, *Stories of Freedom in Black New York* (Boston: Harvard University Press, 2002), 39. Diana DiZerega Wall, Nan A. Rothschild, and Cynthia Copeland, "Seneca Village and Little Africa: Two African American Communities in Antebellum New York City." *Historical Archaeology* 42, no. 1 (2008): 97-98. http://www.jstor.org/stable/25617485.

In the early 1820s, Caribbean-born James Hewlett and Williams Brown, formed the African Grove Theater, the first Black theater company in the United States. Also, living in the area was James McCune Smith, the first African American doctor in the United States. The more prominent Black churches in Five Points included the New Demeter Street Presbyterian Church, led by Reverend Samuel Cornish who founded the church with John Russwurm and Peter Williams co-founders of the *Freedom's Journal*. Founded in March 1827, scholars say this was the first Black-owned newspaper in the United States.

Prominent Black women also lived and worked in Five Points, including Margaret Francis, the president (perhaps a founder) of the African Dorcas Society. Founded in 1828, this group of prominent Black women worked to improve the conditions of life for impoverished residents and Black school children in their community.[4]

It might be easy to assume that Northern Black communities had more wealth than southern ones, but they often had less money. Since White people felt less threatened by Blacks in the South, there were fewer restrictions on their employment. Free Blacks in southern states were able to establish businesses that catered to a White clientele.

For example, in 1853, the First African Baptist Church in Richmond, Va. church received a letter from Eldis C. Lennard asking for "aid for a convention of colored Baptists in the North to preach the gospel to feeble children." The irony of an organization in the North where Blacks were free requesting money from a church where the majority

---

[4] Shane White, *Stories of Freedom in Black New York* (Boston: Harvard University Press, 2002), 73-75; Jonathan Dewberry, "The African Grove Theatre and Company" *Black American Literature Forum* 16, no. 4 (Winter, 1982): 128-31. doi:10.2307/2904218; Leslie M. Harris, *In the Shadow of Slavery: African Americans in New York City, 1626-1863* (Chicago: University of Chicago Press, 2003); Eric Fonner, *Gateway to Freedom: The Hidden History of the Underground Railroad* (New York: W.W. Norton, 2015), 47-51.

of its members were slaves demonstrates the difficult condition in the urban North.[5]

Conditions were so bad in northern cities that some southern African American businessmen remained while sending their families North. It was easier there to receive an education, albeit in segregated schools. For example, George W. Ruffin, while thriving as the proprietor of a prosperous barbershop, sent his entire family to Sussex, Mass. There they interacted with Black ministers, attended school, and enjoyed the benefits of a free-labor society. Ruffin remained in the South running his business until he died in 1863.[6]

Excluded by both law and custom, free African Americans in northern cities were prevented from most common luxuries.

The continuing influx of European immigrants also created new challenges for securing jobs. White employers preferred White laborers. Some immigrants, also carried a strain of racial animosity toward Blacks and used their race to gain economic and social advantages over African Americans. They felt it wasn't in their best interest to associate with Blacks and they tried to keep Blacks out of the best jobs.[7]

Seneca Village: The alternative to Five Points

African Americans who lived in New York City congregated in the traditional Black neighborhoods such as Five Points, Yorkville, or near the ports. The opportunities to purchase land weren't easy because many landowners didn't want to sell land to African Americans, even affluent ones. Since Black men had to own more than $250 in property to vote, prominent Blacks understood that they needed to buy land so

---

[5] *Minutes of the First African Baptist Church of the City of Richmond*, 1842-1858, Library of Virginia, March 6, 1853. Also, see Carey H. Latimore, *The Role of Southern Free Blacks During the Civil War: The Life of Free African Americans in Richmond, Virginia 1850-1876* (Lewiston: Edwin Mellen Press, 2015), 59. Charles C. Andrews, *History of the New York African Free-Schools, from their establishment in 1787 to the present time* (New York: Mahlom Day, 1830), 105, https://books.google.com/books/about/The_History_of_the_New_York_African_Free. html?id=NwpeAAAAcAAJ

[6] Latimore, 126-127.

[7] Latimore, 34.

that they could vote. Therefore, they needed opportunities to purchase land in places like Seneca Village to have a chance to exercise the rights of citizenship.[8]

One of the best opportunities for Blacks to do this happened when speculators purchased large farming tracks near urban centers and subdivided the land. By subdividing larger tracts into smaller ones, speculators could earn money fast and were more willing to sell to Blacks than people who had owned the land for a long time. It was these newer neighborhoods, or nineteenth century suburbs, where African Americans found opportunities to establish communities. This is what happened in Seneca Village when John and Elizabeth Whitehead purchased farmland in an area between West 82nd to West 85th streets between Seventh and Eighth avenues roughly three miles north of Manhattan. This was land outside the city, which meant that there were fewer people living there. It also was less expensive than a similarlysized lot in the city. Because the Whiteheads wanted to make a profit, they probably didn't care who bought the land. With limited access to land, African Americans saw land ownership in Seneca Village as a rare opportunity to attain a reasonable measure of citizenship.

In 1850 only 100 Black men had the right to vote in New York City and at that time, ten of them lived in Seneca Village. This meant that ten percent of the Black voting population in New York City, which then included more than 13,000 residents, lived within a town of less than 300 residents.[9]

Building a community

In September 1825, the Whiteheads sold three lots of land to Andrew Williams, a young African American, for the sum of $125. Although we don't know much about Andrew Williams, we do know that he

---

[8] Livius Drusus, "Seneca Village: The Community that died so that Central Park could Live." Mental Floss, http://mentalfloss.com/article/63039/seneca-village-community-died-so-central-park-could-live (assessed December 8, 2017).

[9] ibid; Roy Rosenzweig and Elizabeth Blackmar, *The Park and the People: A History of Central Park* (Ithaca: Cornel University Press, 1998), 65.

was married with at least three children. From the 1855 New York City census, we learn that Andrew Williams was a coachman, one of the more privileged professions for an African American. This certainly explains his ability to purchase lots and to live a very comfortable life.[10]

Seneca Village wasn't only composed of people interested in individual upward mobility. The residents there also were interested in establishing a community. In New York City, there were a number of community and benevolent associations to help Black people. The African Americans who moved to Seneca Village had a similar spirit. By establishing churches and schools as well as establishing burial grounds, the African Americans who lived in Seneca Village saw it as something more than a place to live. The fact that the Whiteheads sold a number of lots in a short period of time demonstrated how much Black people and community organizations sought these precious opportunities to acquire land. For example, on the same day that Andrew Williams purchased his lot, the trustees of the African Methodist Episcopal Zion Church in Five Points purchased six lots to have space to grow. This proved to be true; they established a church there in 1853. At least one other church, the St. Michaels Episcopal Church opened the All Angels Church by 1850.[11]

AME Zion also bought lots to establish a burial ground for African Americans. Since many graveyards were segregated, Black communities needed land for their own graveyards so African American communities purchased land to provide assistance to Black residents who wanted to purchase a burial plot for their families.

African Americans also saw Seneca Village as an investment. Epiphany Davis, a church trustee, purchased a lot for himself from the Whiteheads on the same day that his church purchased land. Over time, Davis

---

[10] *New York State Census 1855* [database on-line]. Ward 22, Andrew Williams, digital image, Provo, UT, USA, (www.ancestry.com: assessed December 8, 2017).

[11] Rosenzweig and Blackmar, 66 and 71; Diana DiZerega Wall, Nan A. Rothschild, and Cynthia Copeland. "Seneca Village and Little Africa: Two African American Communities in Antebellum New York City." *Historical Archaeology* 42, no. 1 (2008): 101. http://www.jstor.org/stable/25617485; Douglas Martin, "A Village Dies, A Park is Born, New York Times, January 31, 1997, http://www.nytimes.com/1997/01/31/arts/a-village-dies-a-park-is-born.html.

established himself as a major investor in Seneca Village, eventually owning at least twelve lots in the village. Davis also owned land in Yorkville, (York Hill), another area where African Americans developed a community. However, much of York Hill was destroyed to create a city reservoir and that forced some African Americans to move.

As an investor in land and the church, Davis left a substantial legacy to his children who inherited his estate upon his death in 1850. Davis also was committed to Black uplift, as demonstrated by his membership in the New York Society for African Relief, a society devoted to helping the members of their community in need.[12]

Land, church, and burial grounds weren't the only aspects of Black life in Seneca Village. The residents recognized the importance of education, and established a school as part of the AME Zion Church. This endeavor was very successful. Census records from 1850 and 1855 reveal that many African Americans in Seneca Village could read and write. Moreover, roughly 70 percent of Black children attended school. This meant that African American families in Seneca Village valued both education and the church. They viewed both institutions as a crucial investment to ensure the survival of their community.[13]

Despite its residents best efforts, Seneca Village didn't have the population and resources to become a self-sufficient community. The African American families who lived there were dependent upon the city to sustain its operations. Most Blacks who lived in Seneca Village had to find work within the city limits. This reality would have made life somewhat difficult as Blacks were often prohibited from public transportation. However, Anthony Williams and other prominent people in the town owned their own horses. Elite residents like Charles Silven and Josiah Landen either worked as a coachman or had children in those occupations. Coachmen and owners of hack stables would

---

[12] New York City, Wills, vol. 101, 1850-1851, Ephiphany Davis Will, Digital image, page 73 (original text but page 70 according to digital image), (www.ancestry.com: assessed December 8, 2017); Carl Steven Wilder, *In the Company of Black Men: The African Influence on African American Culture in New York City* (New York: NYU Press, 2005 reprint), 101-102.

[13] Wall, Rothschild, and Copeland, 101

have been able to easily travel the distance between Seneca Village and Manhattan. They also could help local residents make the trip downtown to work jobs as waiters or attendants.[14]

Financially, the residents of Seneca Village were well-off compared to African Americans who lived in the downtown area. They found an oasis in Seneca Village and in a sense, established a community that took in their independence. Blacks who purchased land in Seneca Village possessed an entrepreneurial spirit. Some Blacks even purchased land in Seneca Village primarily as an investment. Others built homes in Seneca Village and rented them to other families Some rented out individual rooms in their homes. The residents of Seneca Village knew the value of their land could increase due to its close proximity to the city. They also realized that living away from the city kept them away from the crime and overall impoverished situation of downtown Black communities such as Five Points or Little Africa.

What we learn from Seneca Village

As the town was just getting started, Seneca Village was destroyed as part of a larger citywide plan to create Central Park. Nonetheless, the legacy of education and the church left an imprint on the African American community demonstrating that churches and communities that work together can accomplish great things. As one of the first Black townships in New York, Seneca Village demonstrates the value that Black people placed on land ownership, education, and creating a community. Seneca Village also demonstrates that Black people were more than willing to move to any community that provided an opportunity. Seneca Village was an example that owning businesses and land had the potential to enhance one's ability to participate in the public sphere. Free African Americans like Andrew Williams and Charles Silven, retained their right to vote. They also owned their homes

---

[14] *New York, State Census, 1855* [database on-line]. Ward 22, Charles Silven, digital image, Provo, UT, USA, (www.ancestry.com: assessed December 8, 2017); Leslie Alexander, *African or African American: Black Identity and Political Activism in New York City, 1784-1861* (Chicago: University of Illinois Press, 2011), 56-58.

and probably made extra money by renting rooms to other free African Americans, many who were new residents to the city.[15]

Together they lived a new way of life. It was one that was free from the oppression of slavery and distant from the racism of Northern Whites. They participated in business and politics as free people with their own land. They built their own churches and community organizations. The people of Seneca Village were determined to live life free from the restraints of a racist society.

The repossession of Seneca Village in the late 1850s was yet another example of how local government has the ability to force people off their land to provide for projects servicing elite White communities. Nonetheless, Seneca Village stands as an excellent and early example that Black people could overcome the most arduous impediments to life and still provide a sense of comfort and stability for their families. As demonstrated by the diversity of its Black residents, Black people established a community of free people, freed people, and escaped slaves who united to create a vision of empowerment and self-reliance.

---

[15] *New York, State Census, 1855* [database on-line]. Ward 22, Charles Silven, digital image, Provo, UT, USA, (www.ancestry.com: assessed December 8, 2017).

SWEET HOME, CAPOTE, AND OTHER SETTLEMENTS IN GUADALUPE COUNTY
BUILDING STRONG FAMILIES

> *12 I am sending him—who is my very heart—back to you. 13 I would have liked to keep him with me so that he could take your place in helping me while I am in chains for the gospel. 14 But I did not want to do anything without your consent, so that any favor you do would not seem forced but would be voluntary. 15 Perhaps the reason he was separated from you for a little while was that you might have him back forever— 16 no longer as a slave, but better than a slave, as a dear brother. He is very dear to me but even dearer to you, both as a fellow man and as a brother in the Lord.* (Paul's Letter to Philemon 12-16)

Slavery was a universally known reality in Roman society. The institution encountered far fewer challenges to its legitimacy than American slavery did. Although Paul's letter to Philemon isn't an abolitionist tract, it still holds tremendous significance for Christians because it encourages us to confront the value and dignity of all human life. While Roman law dictated that Philemon's slave Onesimus, who had run away, had no legal rights, Paul's letter transcends it. Paul's letter is a challenge to our society too because, just as his society did, we allow our racial, social, cultural, and class prejudices to determine our opinions of an individual's worth. For Paul, Onesimus' value lies not in the labor he could produce for his master but in his humanity. Although Paul doesn't challenge the legal validity of slavery, he, does something more profound when he asks Philemon to tear down the barriers between him and his slave. We should also take note that Paul doesn't speak in paternal language when he refers to the master/slave relationship, which might signal his belief in a hierarchical relationship between master and slave. Instead, he asks Philemon to see Onesimus "no longer as a slave, but better than a slave, as a dear brother."

Paul sees this relationship as undergirded by his understanding of the Abrahamic covenant fully realized in Christ. As believers, we're all family in Christ. We're descendants of Abraham. When there's an absence of natural family there's the presence of spiritual family.

These ties connect us to one another in an even deeper way than blood and genetics. It is this vision of family that informs our vision of community building. Not only are our own blood relatives important, but we must also look upon the entire community as worthy of the name family. In Paul's mind, the Christian family was heir of the covenant God made with Abraham (Genesis 17:5-9).

Paul understood that by utilizing a language of kinship while asking Philemon to explore his relationship with Onesimus he was truly asking him to see his slave as more than what the world saw. In a society such as ours that is so divided, Paul's letter reveals to us a new type of relationship between people, one where we shouldn't be dictated by worldly things but one where our lives are defined by spiritual principles that confirm the value of all human life.

I am sure that Paul struggled mightily over how to word his plea to Philemon. As we all know, difficult dialogues and conversations when handled without tact and compassion have the potential to divide. We need these conversations because the Black experience in America is one of the least discussed aspects of American life and history. In the African American experience, the path from slavery to freedom included psychological and legal oppression. The Thirteenth Amendment outlawed slavery and subsequent laws and amendments granted African Americans equality in the eyes of the law. However, the peculiar nature and legacy of slavery made the path from slavery to freedom complex. As an increasing urban population today, we might forget that over ninety percent of slaves lived in rural areas and most of their journeys happened in rural spaces. In this chapter, we will spend time focusing on the rural African American experience.

A Peculiar Society: Broken Families

Slavery had a strong impact on South Texas as it did throughout the state. In the years of the Texas Republic, many southern slave owners came to the region often bringing their slaves with them. This led to an increase in the number of Texas slaves. Indeed, between 1836 and 1845, the number of slaves in Texas rose from roughly 5,000 to 30,000. Over the next fifteen years the number of slaves in Texas rose to approximately 180,000. Typically, the slave population came from the upper and lower south. This tremendous migration often broke up many slave families because masters did not always take all family members as they migrated. Slave traders also purchased unknown numbers of slaves and sold them to the gulf south, a region that includes Texas, Mississippi, and Louisiana.[1]

Although we often think of East Texas as the region that contained the majority of Black slaves in Texas, many masters settled in South Texas. For example, the counties of Guadalupe, Caldwell, Wilson, and Gonzales, directly east of San Antonio, had significant slave populations. In Guadalupe County, for example, slaves represented roughly thirty percent of the county's total population. This generated tremendous wealth for slave owners. Because of the wealth slave labor created, along with racial animosity, local White residents did not respond well to the end of the Civil War and emancipation. As a result, they made life difficult for the freed men and women during the immediate postwar years. George W. Smith, head of the Freedmen's Bureau, a government organization that assisted former slaves and others affected by the war, wrote about the majority of White people in Guadalupe county and the surrounding region. They wanted "to keep the Blacks in the same relations to them as when in slavery." Smith also noted that "there are many cases of unfairness toward freedmen in regards to settlements for labor rendered" and that he did not "think

---

[1] Diana Ramey Berry, "In Texas, History of Slavery unique—but not brief," November 8, 2014 MySanAntonio.com, http://www.mysanantonio.com/opinion/commentary/article/In-Texas-history-of-slavery-unique-but-not-5879057.php)

if troops were removed, freed people would get their rights or that civil authorities would give them full protection."[2]

Work contracts were the most significant area of conflict between Blacks and Whites in Guadalupe County. Unfortunately for the freed people, they were often forced by local authorities to enter into contracts of required employment. Local White residents, who needed laborers, strongly supported the contracts. These contracts, however, often ended up being overly advantageous to masters. Former slaves, most of whom were illiterate, often did not know the terms of the contracts. In Guadalupe County, as it was throughout the South, many White employers did not adhere to the contract's requirements. At the same time, the terms of the contract often amounted to little more than slavery. The way Black and White residents negotiated and worked out these contracts ultimately reflected two visions of the new South. Former masters wanted to define freedom in the narrowest manner while former slaves wanted citizenship. The fact that Blacks in Guadalupe brought so many cases to the Freedmen's Bureau demonstrated their unwillingness to silently go along with this abuse.[3]

Some former masters and residents resorted to force to keep Blacks working for them or from exercising their right to choose for whomere they wanted to work. Blacks protested. A freedman from nearby Gonzalez County came to the office to complain of his "sons [still] being held in slavery." Another freedman, Alfred Foster, claimed that his former master kept him in servitude because of debts he incurred while a slave. Other White residents used force to underpay Black workers. Isaac Davis, a former slave master, was accused of threatening a former slave with a gun to ensure that he signed a work contract that would pay him half of what another employer would pay him. This was not

---

[2] Texas, Freedmen's Bureau Field Office Records, 1865-1870," letter of George M. Smith, July 4, 1867 and Letter of Smith to Isaac Davis, January 9, 1867, images, FamilySearch (https://familysearch.org/ark:/61903/3:1:3QS7-L9MX-Q988-1?cc=1989155&wc=94K7-ZJS%3A2666077601%2C266077602: 22 May 2014), Seguin>Roll 26, Letters sent, vol. (153), Jan 1867-Mar 1868, June-Sep. 1868. (Hereafter noted as Seguin Freedmen's Bureau Files)

[3] ibid., for numerous examples please read through Smith's correspondence.

the only accusation against Davis. Another freed person, Jake, charged Davis with forcing him to work without proper compensation.[4]

Portraits of Hope

Although many White residents in Guadalupe did not make life easy for the freed people, there are also examples of tremendous kindness and Christian unity that challenge our interpretations of race relations in the south. Perhaps the most profound example is Florinda Day West's relationship with her former slave, Fillmore. Although we know very little about the faith background of Florinda Day West, it is likely that she was a member of a church considering her background and time period.

Born in Kentucky, Florinda married George Day and migrated to Texas sometime before 1850. The couple did not appear to own slaves before they moved to Texas, but by 1850 they owned one female slave. Considering that Fillmore was born sometime around 1856, it is likely that this slave was his mother. After her husband died in 1859, Florinda made a will that would have manumitted Fillmore upon her death and leave him some property. After the end of slavery, George Smith required that Fillmore be taken from Florinda and sent to his African American father.[5]

One might think that this would end the association between Florinda Day and Fillmore.[6] However, on April 29, 1867, Florinda West appeared before George Smith and the Freedmen's Bureau and, in doing so, provided one of the most beautiful defenses of the sanctity of life and agape love. In her conversation with Smith, West stated that Fillmore was "weakly in body and mind." In modern times we would say that the young child had a physical and intellectual disability. She told Smith

---

[4] Texas, Freedmen's Bureau Field Office Records, 1865-1870," letter of George M. Smith, August 4, 1867, images, FamilySearch (https://familysearch.org/ark:/61903/3:1:3QS7-L9MX-Q988-1?cc=1989155&wc=94K7-ZJS%3A2666077601%2C266077602: 22 May 2014), Seguin>Roll 26, Letters sent, vol. (153), Jan 1867-Mar 1868, June-Sep. 1868

[5] Seguin Freedmen's Bureau Files, Florinda West deposition to George M. Smith April 29, 1867.

[6] Florinda remarried in 1866 to a signer of the Declaration of Texas Independence and former slave owner George West.

that "the father of the boy has taken him away from me and treats him unkindly, refuses to permit him to be educated, and to receive any money or property which I was willing to bestow upon him." West asserted to Smith that she "took good care of him most lately as a mother would of her own." In conclusion, West asked the Bureau to allow her to take Fillmore and to raise him "free from the influence of his father."[7]

Smith pondered the request, seemingly stunned by her affection for the African American child. In dictating his decision, Smith writes that "strange as it may seem [Fillmore] is worshipped by Mrs. West, she having no child of her own" Smith reversed his earlier decision and allowed Mrs. West to "adopt and bring up the child as she would as her own." This was certainly not a legal adoption, but Smith's use of agape language demonstrates his interpretation of the relationship between Fillmore and Mrs. West. West's interest in Fillmore transcended economics, as Fillmore, a child with a disability, could provide her little if any economic benefit.[8]

The relationship between West and Fillmore was not the only one that demonstrated Christian collaboration between the races in Guadalupe County. The life of Hiram Wilson, a Guadalupe business owner and resident of the Capote settlement, is another example. The Capote community was a settlement of African Americans from John M. Wilson's plantation. Wilson, a White Presbyterian minister from North Carolina, arrived in Guadalupe County sometime around 1855 bringing twenty slaves with him. Although he was not skilled in pottery, he provided for the training of some of his male slaves and opened J.M. Wilson Pottery. After slavery's end, he deeded some land to his slaves and apparently sold the business to them. Three of his former slaves, Hiram, James, and Wallace, joined together and formed the Hiram Wilson Pottery Company. According to one author, the company

---

[7] Seguin Freedmen's Bureau Files, Florinda West deposition to George M. Smith April 29, 1867.

[8] Seguin Freedmen's Bureau Files, Florinda West Decision of George M. Smith in Florinda West case, April 29, 1867.

provided "vessels such as crocks, jars, and jugs for food storage and preservation in South Central Texas for 56 years."[9]

According to his descendant Laverne Lewis Britt, Wilson would go on to own about 1,000 acres of land. (Wilson, in praise of Hiram Wilson, 27). Like his former owner, Hiram Wilson entered the ministry and became a leader in the Second Baptist Church in Guadalupe. Wilson also worked closely with the Baptist Missionary Home Society, an organizationthat includednorthern missionaries who wanted to establish churches and help African Americans make the transition to freedom. Reverend Leonard Isley, was one of the society's White ministers who traveled to Guadalupe County immediately after slavery, becoming one of Wilson's mentors.[10]

Wilson and Isley were joined by William Ball, a former free African American from Kentucky. Ball was a graduate of Oberlin College and had served with the Union Army during the Civil War. He moved to Guadalupe around 1870 and worked with the Baptist Missionary Home Society to establish the first schools in the county. The three men also helped found the Guadalupe Baptist Association, uniting the newly established Black Baptist churches throughout the entire region. Wilson, Isley, and Ball also helped found the Negro Baptist College, later named the Guadalupe College, an institution that sought to educate African Americans to be teachers and tradesmen. For many years, Ball served as the college's president .[11]

---

[9] See Marie Blake, Steve Johnson, and Richard Kinz quote in Nola McKey, "The Wilson Pottery," Texas Highways: Travel Magazine of Texas website, http://www.texashighways.com/eat/item/247-the-wilson-potteries)

[10] Laverne Lewis Britt, *In Praise of Hiram Wilson: The Story of a 19th Century Guadalupe Potter* (Bloomington: Xlibris Press, 2005), 29-31.

[11] Andrew Webster Jackson, *A Sure Foundation and a Sketch of Negro Life in Texas* (Houston, 1940); Arwerd Max Moellering, A History of Guadalupe County, Texas (M.A. thesis, University of Texas, 1938); Laverne Lewis Britt, *In Praise of Hiram Wilson: The Story of a 19th Century Guadalupe Potter* (Bloomington: Xlibris Press, 2005); See *Nolan Thompson, "William B. Ball, Handbook of Texas Online,"* accessed December 09, 2017, http://www.tshaonline.org/handbook/online/articles/fba49.

Bridges to building new families

Although the period started rough, things did not stay that way.
By the 1880s, Blacks in Guadalupe County had established strong
communities and settlements. Indeed, Guadalupe included a number
of small settlements, often including less than sixty persons each.
As Smith noted, education was not easy for Blacks in Guadalupe
to procure. Nonetheless, by 1880 much progress had been made,
particularly in the larger settlements. For example, two of the larger
Black settlements in Guadalupe were Sweet Home and Jakes Colony.
According to historians, Sweet Home was settled by former slaves
and the first school was organized in a log cabin. The first mention of a
school at Sweet Home came in the 1870s when it was noted that Sweet
Home "had four months of school with Ellen Clark as teacher." This was
more months of education compared to the other settlements such as
Zion Hill or Randolph that only held school for three months. In 1924,
residents of Sweet Home raised enough money to receive additional
funding from the Rosenwald Foundation to establish a Rosenwald
Trade School. In addition to this school, there were eventually five other
Rosenwald Schools in Guadalupe County, demonstrating the residents'
dedication to pursuing their own education.[12]

The Beloved Community

Toward the end of his life, Hiram Wilson founded a church on his land.
That church still stands today and services are held there. In the church,
there's a picture of Reverends Wilson, Isley, and Bell together. These
three men--a former slave, a White man, and a free African American--
represent the same vision of community that the Apostle Paul wrote
to in his letter to Philemon. Today, the contributions of these three
men continue in the churches they created, the Guadalupe Baptist

---

[12] Josephine S. Etlinger, *Sweetest You Can Find: Life in Eastern Guadalupe County, Texas, 1851–1951* (San
Antonio: Watercress, 1987), 182; For a list of all Rosenwald Schools throughout the country please consult the
Rosenwald searchable database at Fisk University, http://rosenwald.fisk.edu.

Association they helped to found, the memories of the college they started, and the people their legacy inspired.

Although Guadalupe County's Black community has less members today than it did in the early twentieth century, the Black residents of the county have tremendous pride in the churches and schools their ancestors created. In Guadalupe County, many African Americans still define themselves by the settlement their ancestors lived in after slavery. Such historical memory is a wonderful legacy and reveals that knowledge of one's past provides hope for a glorious future.

TULSA, OK
SKILLS TO BUILD

*The Egyptians urged the people to hurry and leave the country.
"For otherwise," they said, "we will all die!"* [34] *So the people
took their dough before the yeast was added, and carried it on
their shoulders in kneading troughs wrapped in clothing.* [35] *The
Israelites did as Moses instructed and asked the Egyptians for
articles of silver and gold and for clothing.* (Exodus 12:33-35)

On the morning of June 1, 1921, Black residents in Greenwood, Tulsa
awoke to the sight of their entire community in flames. That night
and into the morning, mobs of White residents of Tulsa crossed the
railroad tracks that divided Tulsa's Black and White communities with
the intent to destroy everything within sight. By the time the National
Guard arrived to put the riot down, there was little left of Greenwood's
more than 30 city blocks. Moreover, roughly 300 Black people were
dead, thousands injured, and 11,000 residents homeless. Homeless
and destitute, local officials forced African American residents into tent
cities where they remained until they could rebuild their community,
something they would have to do without any help from the local, state,
or federal government.[1]

Rebuilding Greenwood, which had once stood as a symbol of Black
progress, wouldn't be easy. Not only did residents have to physically
recover but they also had to overcome the emotional and psychological
trauma the riot left behind. Making matters worse, in the wake of the
most destructive race riot in American history, not one White person
was ever convicted of any crime perpetrated that night. Indeed, the

---

[1] Tim Madigan, *The Burning: Massacre, Destruction, and the Tulsa Race Riot of 1921* (New York: Thomas Dunne
Books, 2001), 131-132

committee appointed in the aftermath and tasked with determining the reasons for the riot, maliciously and erroneously claimed that African Americans were guilty of inciting the riot that destroyed their entire community. The committee concluded that the assault of a White woman, an unproven accusation, and the local Black residents' confrontation of a lynch mob that gathered at the local courthouse where the accused was located earlier in the day caused the riot. Even though Black residents of Greenwood never received justice they didn't let this setback destroy their dreams. Although it took years to recover and, indeed, many individuals and their families never fully recovered, the most important lesson to be learned from Greenwood isn't that White terrorists destroyed an entire community, but it is the fact that Black people had the spirit and determination not only to build their own "Black Wall Street" but they had the spirit to rebuild it when racism destroyed it.[2]

A Community of Builders

One of the most noteworthy things about Greenwood is how quickly Black people built the community. The history of Black people in Oklahoma goes back to the 1830s with the forced removal of Native Americans to the Oklahoma Territory. Many Indians brought their Black slaves with them. The end of the Civil War freed these slaves who now had the opportunity to determine their economic and social destinies. Additionally, the United States government gradually reduced the amount of territory for the five Indian tribes and offered the land to settlers. In 1889, the first of the Oklahoma land rushes happened where unassigned land was given to prospective homesteaders. Included in this group of homesteaders were many African Americans who saw this as an opportunity to build a life of their own.[3]

As a result of available land and the opportunity to escape the worst aspects of racism in the deep South, the Black population of Oklahoma rose considerably. In 1890 the Black population was 3,000.

---

[2] Madigan, 43-45; 89-98

[3] Madigan, 14-15; Christopher Klein, "Remembering the Oklahoma Land Rush," Last Modified, April, 22, 2014. http://www.history.com/news/the-oklahoma-land-rush-125-years-ago

Ten years later it was more than 50,000. During that time, Tulsa, however, remained a very small town. This changed in 1905 when the discovery of oil in Tulsa led to a population boom. By 1910, Tulsa had a population of 18,000. Ten years later, it rose to more than 70,000. The Black population of Tulsa was 2,000 in 1910, and by 1920, stood at roughly 8,800. By 1920, the community had two theaters, more than 100 businesses, a hospital, numerous churches, and a variety of other fraternal and mutual aid societies.[4]

This hearkens to the story of the Israelites' readiness to leave Egypt in Exodus chapter twelve. They took not only gold and silver from the Egyptians, but also a readiness to build a new life for themselves. They had three particular skills that any people hoping to build community must have: worship in the wilderness, a readiness mentality, and financial planning. You can see these different skills in Greenwood residents as they built churches, businesses, and fraternal organizations.

Greenwood's location in the northern part of the city, some distance from the city's core, provided an escape from White racism. Segregation in Tulsa allowed Black businesses to thrive in an environment that forced Black people not only to promote Black businesses but also attend Black schools, churches, fraternal organizations, and other Black institutions. Even though segregation meant that African Americans supported Black institutions, many Blacks still worked in the city's southside which was the White side of town.[5]

The early African American settlers in Tulsa were similar to the Black people who moved to Mound Bayou. These men and women sought opportunities and land to establish a settlement away from the virulent racism of the South. It was not unusual for the early Black residents to have moved several times before coming to Tulsa, a sign that residents

---

[4] "Table 37. Oklahoma-Race and Hispanic Origins for Selected Large Cities and Other Places: Earliest Census," United States Department of Commerce Census Bureau, assessed December 5, 2017. https://www.census.gov/population/www/documentation/twps0076/OKtab.pdf

[5] James M. Smallwood, "Segregation," *The Encyclopedia of Oklahoma History and Culture*, www.okhistory.org (accessed December 07, 2017)

were willing to travel long distances to pursue their dreams. Other residents, however, had been chased out their previous homes by racism. O.W. Gurley was probably the first Black to arrive in Tulsa. Born in 1866, Gurley, a son of slaves, grew up in Alabama and later moved to Arkansas. O.W. Gurley became a teacher but wanted more for himself and was drawn by the opportunity to acquire land in Oklahoma. He moved to Oklahoma and was part of the land rush of 1893. By 1900, Gurley lived in Perry, Oklahoma, and operated a merchant store. The discovery of oil in Tulsa provided him with another opportunity for success. Given an opportunity to purchase land on the city's northside, he recognized that the land he purchased could be zoned and sold to Black people. Since the Oklahoma constitution barred all types of racial integration, from housing to telephones, Gurley designated the area for African Americans, creating Greenwood. He also took many steps to help build the community and establish Tulsa as a place of opportunity for African Americans. A keen businessman, he understood that segregation meant that Black people needed a place to live close enough to the downtown area for work. He also understood that businesses would come to Greenwood if it became a sustainable community. Gurley initiated this process by constructing a hotel, opening a mercantile store, and starting a meat market. Gurley's hotel also served as a permanent residence for recent immigrants to Tulsa. For example, in 1920, there were five renters living in his hotel. Gurley was always willing to experiment, and after losing all of his property during the riot, he and his wife moved to Los Angeles and built another hotel for Black people.[6]

Tulsa's early African American residents cultivated good relationships with the local police and government officials. Gurley, also a deputy sheriff, was a skilled networker who was well respected by the local political elite. With his connections he had more power than many Blacks could ever enjoy, even if these privileges could and would

---

[6] ibid; Madigan, 17-20; 1880 U.S. Census, *Vaugine, Jefferson, Arkansas*; Roll: *48*; Family History Film: *1254048*; Page: *136A*; Enumeration District: 149, John Gurley, digital image, (www.ancestry.com: assessed December 8, 2017); 1920 U.S. Census, *Tulsa, Tulsa, Oklahoma*; Roll: *T625_1487*; Page: *5B*; Enumeration District: *256*, www.ancestry.com: assessed December 8, 2017)

eventually be revoked when he lost everything during the riot. For example, in 1916 an incident occurred at his hotel that demonstrated just how much clout he had with local authorities. White men entered his hotel "looking for immoral purposes." Emma Gurley, his wife and hotel manager, informed the men that this was not that type of hotel. Upset with her response, the men assaulted Emma Gurley, eventually leading to an altercation with her husband. Even though Gurley had physically attacked White men, he was not prosecuted. Gurley's connections to the local White elite were shared by other Black Tulsanites, particularly the earlier settlers. Jake Dillard, who established the first Black school in the city, was another local networker and was one of the biggest promoters of the Democratic Party. As a reward for his service to the Democratic Party, he was nominated Justice of the Peace for his district. He won in the election, becoming the first elected Black official in the city. He also was a police officer for many years.[7]

Because there was more land available in Tulsa's northside, other real estate investors such as Thomas Gentry flocked to the city with the idea of purchasing larger tracts of land and subdividing them. Born in 1879 in Kansas, Thomas Gentry moved several times before coming to Oklahoma. In 1904 he arrived in Tulsa securing a job as a porter at the Brady Hotel. During the three years he worked at the hotel, he established a strong relationship with Tate Brady, the proprietor and owner of the hotel. This relationship continued even after Gentry opened his own businesses. By 1918, Brady purchased and subdivided a large plot of land called Gurley Hill. Gentry became an agent for this property and offered this property to African Americans.[8]

---

[7] "Insults Colored Woman: Gets Kicked Out," *The Tulsa Star* (Tulsa, OK), Nov. 11, 1916, From the Library of Congress website Chronicling America: Historic American Newspapers, http://chroniclingamerica.loc.gov/lccn/sn86064118/1916-11-11/ed-1/seq-1/. In order to save space all future sources in this chapter from this database will be listed under Chronicling America.; Judge Jake Dillard Brought the Bacon Home," *The Tulsa Star* (Tulsa, OK), Nov. 9, 1918, Chronicling America, http://chroniclingamerica.loc.gov/lccn/sn86064118/1918-11-09/ed-1/seq-3/
; "Local News in and Around Town," *The Tulsa Star* (Tulsa, OK), Aug. 8, 1913, Chronicling America, http://chroniclingamerica.loc.gov/lccn/sn86064118/1913-08-08/ed-1/seq-2/

[8] From Porter to Land Lord: Success of Well Known Tulsan Should be Inspiration to Others," *The Tulsa Star* (Tulsa, OK), Dec. 22, 1917, Chronicling America, http://chroniclingamerica.loc.gov/lccn/sn86064118/1917-12-22/ed-1/seq-1

Gentry saved enough money during his three-year employment with Brady to purchase a lot in Greenwood and opened a bar. The Oquawka was referred to as a classy bar and billiard hall that was "one of the biggest and best of its kind in the city." He also owned a property at 108 North Greenwood that served as a mall where business owners would rent spaces. Gentry also rented houses to local residents.[9]

Black women were also able to build a life of their own in Tulsa and established numerous businesses. Daisy Scott, an African American woman from Little Rock, moved to Tulsa with her husband.She owned and operated an artistic millinery and seamstress business. She also was the *Tulsa Star's* cartoonist. The riot had a devastating effect on her life. According to the 1930 census, she was relegated to working as a janitor in the years after the riot. Another African American woman, Anna Warren, was one of the most prominent women in Tulsa. Born in Mississippi, her husband was a clerk in a hotel but died before 1920. Warren, however, established and operated a beauty parlor. She was a member of the local business league and a member of the executive board of the Humane Society. Warren was appointed sanitary officer by Tulsa's mayor.[10]

Organizations and Community: Moral Uplift

Greenwood was much more than a place where individuals went to make their fortune. What made Greenwood special was Black people working together and pooling their resources to build community. O.W. Gurley, mentioned earlier, not only made his fortune by investing in real estate, he also constructed the building that would become the Vernon Chapel Methodist AME Church. By 1921, Vernon Methodist was

[9] *The Tulsa Star* (Tulsa, OK), December 22, 1917, Chronicling America, http://chroniclingamerica.loc.gov/lccn/sn86064118/1917-12-22/ed-1/seq-1/
The Tulsa Star (Tulsa, OK), May 9, 1913, http://chroniclingamerica.loc.gov/lccn/sn86064118/1913-05-09/ed-1/seq-5/

[10] *The Tulsa Star* (Tulsa, OK), February 14, 1920, Chronicling America, http://chroniclingamerica.loc.gov/lccn/sn86064118/1920-02-14/ed-1/seq-1/; *The Tulsa Star* (Tulsa, OK), Chronicling America, December 12, 1914, http://chroniclingamerica.loc.gov/lccn/sn86064118/1914-12-12/ed-1/seq-1/; *The Tulsa Star* (Tulsa, OK), April 11, 1913, Chronicling America, http://chroniclingamerica.loc.gov/lccn/sn86064118/1913-04-11/ed-1/seq-1

one of the largest churches in Greenwood. It was particularly active in promoting its youth and in home missions. The church had an active Junior League and Epworth League for their youth and young adults. Some of the other larger churches in Greenwood included the First Baptist and Mt. Zion Baptist churches. There was also a Methodist Church and a Christian Methodist Episcopal church in Tulsa.[11]

Many fraternal organizations and lodges also existed in Tulsa. One of the most important fraternal organizations was the Knights of the Pythias, which, although it was not as prominent in Tulsa as it was in Jackson Ward (Richmond City), still had a strong presence. The Eastern Star Lodge and Odd Fellows also had a strong following in Greenwood. Perhaps the largest organization in the city, however, was the Grand Lodge United Brothers of Friendship and Sisters of the Mysterious Ten Lodge. This lodge was another benevolent association that provided services for its members. Formed in Louisville, Kentucky, in 1861 by a group of slaves and free African Americans, the United Brothers of Friendship was only for African Americans, a fact that separated it from the other large fraternal organizations. Within a few years of its founding, the Sisters of the Mysterious Ten Lodge became the women's auxiliary to the group. The Sisters held conventions, inspired by the ideas of moral uplift, and provided its members with insurance. By 1880, the Lodge instituted an insurance department so that it could work as a mutual aid society. By 1918, the organization had become large in Tulsa and was pressing hard to become the largest fraternal organization in the city. The editor of the *Tulsa Star*, apparently a member, wrote that the Negro "is seeing the wisdom of uniting with the Negro, and at each meeting the leaders work together."[12]

---

[11] Scott Ellisworth, "The Tulsa Race Riot," in Tulsa Race Riot: A Report by the Oklahoma Commission to Study the Race Riot of 1921, The Oklahoma Commission to Study the Race Riot of 1921 (CreateSpace Independent Publishing Platform, 2001), 60;

[12] William H. Gibson, *History of the United brothers of friendship and Sisters of the Mysterious Ten* (Louisville: The Bradley and Gilbert Company, 1897), 46-60 and iv, https://books.google.com/books?id=2IMMAQAAMAAJ&print sec=frontcover&source=gbs_ge_summary_r&cad=0#v=onepage&q&f=false, assessed December 7, 2017; *The Tulsa Star* (Tulsa, OK), February 2, 1918;

Greenwood's Black Chamber of Commerce also helped to unite Black business leaders. The chamber took an active role in policing the morality of the community, probably in an effort to ensure the White business community that the Black community couldn't be stereotyped. The chamber attempted to establish strong relationships with the local police, even though most of the officers policing the Black community were White. The chamber worked to stop the perceived growing influence of Tulsa's underground and even declared "war" against it in 1913. In particular the chamber was concerned about places like the "Supple Socks" places where prostitutes, gambling, and drinking occurred. The chamber appointed a committee on law and order to "improve the moral conditions of this city." Two weeks later, the major African American bar in town, the Supple Socks, closed . The chamber worked closely with ministers, lawyers, real estate agents, and newspaper editors.[13]

Rebuilding

At the time of the riots, Black residents in Tulsa had built a "Black Wall Street." Even though it is amazing what Black residents did in a very short period of time, it is probably even more inspiring what they accomplished after the riot. Without any real assistance, Black residents, some who had been slaves, rebuilt their community. Perhaps there is no better example of that spirit than the history of Mount Zion Baptist Church. In 1909, the congregation held services in a school. But by 1916, they had raised enough money to begin to look for a permanent location. A $50,000 loan help them complete construction on April 4, 1921. Less than two months later, however, the riot reduced the church to rubble. But the congregation didn't lose their faith and continued to meet and worked diligently to pay off the debt. They made a temporary church within the rubble of the old church. Seventeen years later, they initiated new plans to construct a new building. By

---

[13] *The Tulsa Star* (Tulsa, OK), July 18, 1913, chronicling America, http://chroniclingamerica.loc.gov/lccn/sn86064118/1913-07-18/ed-1/seq-1/;
The Tulsa Star (Tulsa, OK), August 8, 1913, chronicling America, http://chroniclingamerica.loc.gov/lccn/sn86064118/1913-08-08/ed-1/seq-1/

1948, the new church building was completed. This church building still stands on the same ground and the remnants of the old church remain at its foundation.[14]

Other Black residents relied on their past experiences to rebuild. Born enslaved, Townshend Jackson had once organized a Black militia and was eventually invited to become a member of the Memphis police force. His affluence, perhaps, led to a mob attempt to destroy his home. Before the mob could arrive, however, Jackson and his whole family had left the state to pursue new opportunities in Oklahoma. In Oklahoma, the Jackson family thrived. Townshend's son, Andrew, attended Meharry Medical College and became a doctor. After graduation, he established himself in Tulsa. The elder Townshend served his community as a member of a local fraternity. The Greenwood riot almost destroyed his family as rioters murdered his son and destroyed all of his property. In the twilight of his life, forced to live in a tent city, Townshend demonstrated his spirit and he started cutting hair to earn money to start rebuilding again.[15]

Some Blacks left Tulsa to rebuild their lives. Andrew Smitherman, the editor of the *Tulsa Star*, left immediately after the riot. Nonetheless, he didn't leave his dreams behind in Tulsa. He first moved to Springfield, Massachusetts and eventually ended up in Buffalo, New York where he founded another newspaper the *Empire Star*. He remained newspaper's editor until his death in 1961.[16]

These different Tulsanites serve as an example of the skills used by the Israelites after their freedom from slavery:

- worship in the wilderness

- a readiness mentality

---

[14] Cathy Ambler, Mount Zion Baptist Church, Tulsa, Oklahoma. National Register of Historic Places Nomination Form. Oklahoma Historical Society, September 5, 2008; Madigan, 155-157.

[15] Madigan, 7-8 and 173-184

[16] Larry O'Dell, "Smitherman, Andrew J.," *The Encyclopedia of Oklahoma History and Culture*, www.okhistory.org (accessed December 07, 2017)

- financial planning

With these skills they overcame the effects of racism and the lack of resources due to the devastation of their community.

Conclusion:

Greenwood stands today because its residents have always been builders. They used their skills to establish relationships with each other and even outside their communities. Whether it was building organizations, building families, or establishing businesses, Black Tulsanites proved adaptable enough to take the necessary risks to adopt successful strategies that allowed them to seize their dreams. Even the riot of 1921 couldn't destroy the spirit of a people dedicated to progress and building their community.

HAYTI: DURHAM, NORTH CAROLINA
BUILDING GOD'S HOUSE

It is a peculiar sensation, this double-consciousness, this sense of always looking at one's self through the eyes of others, of measuring one's soul by the tape of a world that looks on in amused contempt and pity. One ever feels his twoness--an American, a Negro; two souls, two thoughts, two unreconciled strivings; two warring ideals in one dark body, whose dogged strength alone keeps it from being torn asunder.[1]

In the years following emancipation, many African Americans wandered in an allegorical wilderness. Almost all of the towns we have discussed up to this point were created by Black people as they picked up their possessions in search of a new life. This African American exodus symbolized the hopes and dreams of a people struggling to overcome their own double consciousness.

As they founded these towns, African Americans wanted sustainable communities and a space to express their own identity and being. The W.E.B. Du Bois quote spoke of the double consciousness that African Americans have. One concludes that within the Black American soul lay all the literal and symbolic struggles of an outcast living in a society of privilege. Thrust away from acceptance and a true homeland, both in the motherland and their new home, Black people embarked on new journeys in their search for Canaan. Hayti, a Black town in Durham, North Carolina, from its inception in the period of the Civil War through World War II shined as a community where Black people created a community of purpose.

---

[1] W.E.B. Dubois, *The Souls of Black Folk* (Chicago: A.C. McClurg & Co, 1909), 3.

In the Beginning

Durham's founding was similar to Mound Bayou and Greenwood. During the Antebellum Period, the southern states lagged behind the northern ones in industrialization. Transportation in the region was often nonexistent. Nevertheless, during the 1850s, some areas in the upper South including what became Durham took steps toward industrialization and improving their infrastructure.

Bartlett Durham, a large landowner, donated a small piece of his land to the North Carolina Railroad, a railroad connected North Carolina's coastal plains region with its Piedmont region. Durham Station, the area of his land he donated to the railroad, became one of the station points. In 1869, the General Assembly of North Carolina incorporated the town of Durham.[2]

Durham remained a small town in its formative years. Its lush lands, green scenery, relatively low elevation, as well as its fertile soils, made it an attractive place to live for Whites and Blacks. In 1866, a group of African Americans Christians met at the home of Margaret Faucette, an African American woman and wife of a local farmer. This group would become the First Missionary Baptist Church, and later, the Rock Missionary Baptist Church. Their services were held on Elm Street and then Fayetteville Street, the center of Hayti.[3]

In 1868, Edian Markham, an African American missionary, arrived in Durham to establish an African American Methodist church. He purchased land near Fayetteville and Pettigrew streets and founded a church. Markham was an educated man and it is thought that he alsostarted a school on the property. The church, initially named Union Bethel AME church, was later changed to St. Joseph AME church.[4]

---

[2] William K. Boyd, *The Story of Durham, City of the New South* (Durham: North Carolina, Duke University Press), 25-8.

[3] "History of White Rock Baptist Church," White Rock Baptist Church, assessed December 5, 2017. http://www.Whiterockbaptistchurch.org/history

[4] Louis Alston, The History of St. Joseph's AME Church and the St. Joseph's Historic Foundation," *Hayti Heritage Center*, assessed December 5, 2017. . . . . https://hayti.org/about-us/our-history.

In the story of Hayti's founding, we see the central place of the church. It is through the church and its network of people, families, and resources that many of our institutions have been built. Nowhere is that more clearly seen than in the neighborhood of Hayti. The churches were the bedrock of the community. They were the first places that were built. This shows the importance of worship and trust in God in the lives of the formerly enslaved people.

Tobacco and the Trinity

Even though there was a small Black community in Durham by 1870, the decade of the 1870s witnessed the development of the town into a major industrial center. This was caused by the rise of the tobacco industry.

After the Civil War left Richmond City, Virginia in flames, tobacco manufacturers looked for new land. By the early 1870s, W.T. Blackwell established his tobacco warehouses in Durham that produced Bull Durham smoking tobacco. The work done in Blackwell's tobacco factory typically required very little skill. This created jobs for African Americans, albeit low-paying ones, stemming, packing, and sorting tobacco.

During the same period, George Washington Duke and his family came to Durham to set up their tobacco warehouse.W. Duke and Sons processed cigarettes rather than simply producing tobacco which made smoking easier. By the 1880s, the Duke family had become the largest cigarette manufacturer in the country, producing jobs for Blacks from the countryside.[5]

Even though Durham's Black community centered around Hayti, this wasn't the only place African Americans lived. Other residential locations included a number of small communities throughout Durham,

---

[5] Patrick Porter, "Advertising in the Early Cigarette Industry: W. Duke, Sons and Company of Durham." North Carolina Historical Review 48 (January 1971): 31-43;
Walter Weare, *Black Business in the New South: A Social History of the NC Mutual Life* (Durham, NC: Duke University Press, 1993), 43-44.

mostly in the Southern portions of the city. These areas often had the worst drainage and sat on low-elevated lands, making them prone to flooding. Farming cycles also led African Americans to migrated from countryside. In North Carolina the typical farming season occurred during the spring, summer, and early fall. Family incomes could also be supplemented by travelling to Durham to work on a short-term basis in the tobacco warehouses during offseason.

The lure of jobs and opportunity led to increases in the city's Black population. Between 1890 and 1910, the Black community in Durham rose from 1,859 to 6,869. By 1910, the Black population was roughly 38 percent of the city's population. According to one study, there were at least eleven separate Black communities in Durham, but Hayti was by far the most important and largest. The more prosperous and stable African Americans families lived in Hayti, a community that had everything Black people needed to survive on a day to day basis. A prominent resident of Hayti was Fannie Rosser, a single Black women who was an employee of the Mutual Insurance Company, and a real estate broker and investor.[6]

Building a Community

As they did during the antebellum years, Black people with skills had an opportunity to prosper. Even though professional men like Dr. Aaron Moore and Charles Clinton Spaulding became prominent in Durham, the most assessable means for Black people to increasetheir status was through a marketable skill.

The Amey family, one of the most important families involved in education in Durham, represented a typical Black family in Hayti. Cornelius Amey, born before the end of slavery, owned and operated

---

[6] John N. Ingham, "Building Businesses, Creating Communities: Residential Segregation and the Growth of African American Business in Southern Cities, 1880-1915." *The Business History Review* 77, no. 4 (2003): 660. http://www.jstor.org/stable/30041232; John Kellogg, ""Negro Urban Clusters in the Postbellum South." *Geographical Review* 67, no. 3 (1977): 310-21. doi:10.2307/213725.
; Anne M. Valk and Leslie Brown, *Living with Jim Crow: African American women and memories of the segregated South* (New York: Palgrave Macmillan, 2010), 24

a blacksmith shop in Hayti. His son, Clinton, was an employee of the Mechanics and Farmers Bank and later an instructor and business manager at the North Carolina Central College. His wife, Mildred, came from Gastonia, North Carolina and was a principal (supervisor) of a rural Jeanes school. The Jeanes Foundation was an organization that set up schools throughout the rural south. [7]

Many Black people in Hayti not only maintained their status over the period of Hayti's ascent, but also increased it. Much of this has to do with the establishment of an African American business elite in Hayti that maintained very cordial relationships with White businessmen. Although race relations in Durham reflected the impulses of Jim Crow, the community did have a number of White philanthropists and benefactors of the Black community including the Duke and Carr families. Both of these families had ties to the tobacco industry and employed African Americans in their factories. These relationships protected Hayti from some of the more visceral racial hostilities. Such incidents included the Wilmington, North Carolina insurrection where a White mob overturned a democratically elected Republican government in 1898. In the early years of Durham's ascendancy, these relationshipshelped spur Black economic development.

Promoting Economic Nationalism

Although it might be natural to view the interracial relationships between Durham's business communities as more beneficial to White businessmen, such a conclusion is shortsighted. Hayti's most active economic and social leaders including John Merrick, Dr. Aaron Moore, and Charles Clinton Spaulding, all maintained strong relationships with Durham's White business elite. No African American was more able to cultivate beneficial relationships with prominent White citizens than John Merrick. His life and accomplishments demonstrate his skill in

---

[7] Robert C. Kenzer, *Enterprising Southerners: Black Economic Success in North Carolina 1865-1915* (Charlottesville: The University of Virginia Press, 1997), 124; 1920 U.S. Census, *Crowder Mountain, Gaston, North Carolina*; Roll: *T625_1299*; Page: *10A*; Enumeration District: *75, Mildred Wellman; digital image, Ancestry.com (http://www. ancestry.com: assessed December 5, 2017.*

mastering the art of collaboration during the era of Jim Crow. Born a slave in Sampson County, a county roughly 95 miles south of Durham, Merrick did not know his father. A man without much formal education, by the age of twelve he along with his family had moved to Chapel Hill where he worked in a brickyard. By the time he was twenty, Merrick lived in Raleigh, North Carolina and worked as a shoe shiner in W.G. Otey's barbershop. Otey made a good living from his business and his barbershop was a meeting spot for prominent White businessmen. Here Merrick initiated relationships with White businessmen as well as Black barbers, including John Wright. Merrick and Wright became friends and business partners. Wright later wrote, "After some time I was persuaded by Colonel W.T. Blackwell, Mr. J.S. Carr, Mr. W. Duke and other White friends to come to Durham and go into business. ... Our place of business contained three chairs at the beginning and later we added five more."[8]

Establishing Connections

Merrick also established connections with Durham's Black professional, religious, and business elite. Most important was Dr. Aaron Moore, perhaps Merrick's closest associate and friend. Born during the Civil War to a free African American family in rural North Carolina, Moore attended Shaw University in nearby Raleigh, North Carolina and was eventually certified as a medical doctor. He moved to Durham in the late 1880s, becoming the town's first Black physician.[9]

Moore initiated a number of projects in Hayti that enhanced life for its residents, specifically Lincoln Hospital and the Colored Library. The first project that Moore spearheaded was a Black pharmacy. Moore brought a group of African American businessmen together for this venture, including Robert B. Fitzgerald and W.G. Pearson. The pharmacy

---

[8] Andrew R. McCants, "John Merrick: A Biological Sketch" (Durham: The Seeman Printery, 1920), 32.

[9] "In Search of Dr. Aaron McDuffie Moore," Shaw University, assessed December 5, 2017. http://www.shawu.edu/In_Search_of_Dr__Aaron_McDuffie_Moore.aspx; "Aaron McDuffie Moore, History Beneath our Feet," Museum of Durham History, assessed December 5, 2017. http://museumofdurhamhistory.org/beneathourfeet/people/Moore-MAaron

provided medicines for Black people while also creating jobs. Two of the early supporters of the pharmacy, J.A. Dodson and J.E. Shepard, were pharmacists from Shaw University, Moore's alma mater. Years later, Moore along with Merrick, Charles Clinton Spaulding, and W.G. Preston, opened a second Black drug store in Hayti. As it was in the earlier pharmacy, this one created jobs and provided experience to young pharmacists right out of college.[10]

Perhaps, Moore's greatest legacy, however, was Lincoln Hospital. When it opened in 1901, the hospital was the only Black hospital in Durham. Years later he wrote the following about the founding of the hospital.

> "The movement for a colored hospital was started by me in 1898. I worked hard to arouse the colored and White people in the interest of such an institution for our city, and gradually they began to respond. We were especially endeavoring to win the encouragement of the Duke family. Dr. A.G. Carr, my good friend, was the family doctor for the Dukes, John Merrick was the family barber, W.H. Armstrong was the butler and Mrs. Addie Evans was the cook. I kept in touch with all these persons and we had a fairly good opportunity to see that the matter did not grow cold. All these persons help to win the favor of our friends and benefactors, the Dukes, but I suppose Dr. Carr and Mr. Merrick were more largely responsible for the generous gifts we received."[11]

Interracial Collaboration

Moore's reflections demonstrate not only the depth of interracial collaboration in supporting the hospital but it also reveals how he viewed interracial collaboration through a Black nationalist frame. Moore also demonstrated his nationalist tendencies through his donation of property for the Colored Library in 1913. He envisioned the library as an

---

[10] McCants, 56-7.
[11] McCants, 46-7.

opportunity for young Black children to learn about their history and to contribute to the local public schools.[12]

Hayti's professional and business elite worked hard to meet the needs of its Black residents. Insurance was one area of focus. They understood that having access to insurance and death insurance was particularly important for Black people. In North Carolina and throughout the United States, the reluctance of White-owned life insurance companies to sell life insurance plans to African Americans threatened financial ruin for many middle-class families when a family member died.

In 1883, John Merrick and four other African American businessmen including John Wright, purchased the rights to the Royal Knights of King David, a religious fraternal organization in Georgia. The organization wasn't only a fraternal organization but, similar to many fraternal organizations of the period, provided life insurance to its members. Members of the order included W.G. Pearson, a school principal. In 1920, members of the order helped establish the Fraternal Bank and Trust Company. [13]

A Pivotal Organization

To serve the needs for the larger Black community, Black leaders in Hayti came to believe that the community needed a larger organization. In 1898, seven Black leaders, including four founders of the Royal Knights, created the North Carolina Mutual and Provident Association. Although the first attempt failed, soon after Merrick, Moore, and Spaulding reorganized the company and appointed Spaulding the manager. Spaulding envisioned the association in the broadest terms possible and he wanted the company to exist not only in Durham but throughout the nation.

---

[12] McCants, 60-61.
[13] McCants, 44-46.

To accomplish this goal, the company employed agents to sell insurance. T.J. Russell was one of the first employees, on a part-time basis. As an employee of a tobacco factory, Russell helped promote the company to tobacco employees. At the same time, this allowed Russell to earn extra money. Eventually, he decided to quit his $6 a week job at the tobacco warehouse. His old employer offered to double his salary but the mutual company offered him $15 per week. Russell's experience wasn't alone.

The employees of this business made much more than the workers in the tobacco factories and did not experience workplace oppression. For example, according to Leslie Brown and Anne Valk, while new employees at the tobacco warehouses could earn "$2.50 per week in 1915, the Mutual started its clerical staff at $30.00 per month and promised regular increases." By 1920 the company was the largest and most successful Black business in the nation, offering plans to Black people throughout the country.[14]

Bank for the Community

Black residents of Hayti also had a bank. Having a Black bank certainly enhanced the Black community's financial portfolio. The bank provided credit for the purchase of real estate and led the way for the creation of other businesses.

According to McCants, the idea for creating a bank came from many of the leaders involved in the fraternity and insurance agency. McCants writes that according to Dr. Aaron Moore:

> "Professor E.A. Johnson and Dr. Pope, of Raleigh, came to Durham one night in 1907 to work up a building and loan association. We called a meeting of the leading men of the town in order to discuss the matter. It was soon evident from the turn of the meeting that the persons present wanted a bank rather than a building and

---

[14] McCants, 72-3; Brown and Valk, 25

loan association. Soon after this R.B. Fitzgerald, John Merrick and others began to show activity toward establishing a bank."[15]

Robert B. Fitzgerald, was a brick maker from a prominent free African American family in Delaware, perhaps the wealthiest Black family in the state. A Civil War veteran, he moved to Durham shortly after the war. Moore and Fitzgerald took the reins to find investors for the bank and eventually, the Mechanics and Farmers Bank was incorporated in 1908. As a sign of the close ties between the Durham business community and the bank, the bank was initially located in the office of the Royal Knights of King David.[16]

Hayti's Future

Hayti continued to thrive through World War II as the community boasted active churches, a movie theater, a hospital, community organizations such as the YMCA and YWCA, and many Black-owned businesses.

For a few years, Hayti was also the home to the only Black-owned and operated textile mill in the country. However, urban renewal and integration helped to destroy much of what Black residents built. By the late 1950s the city began to demolish many of Hayti's historical buildings. The creation of Interstate 147 further divided the Black community by razing historic landmarks and splitting the community.[17]

Today there is hope for renewal, however. The Hayti Heritage Center stands on the grounds of the old St. Joseph's Church. Some of the other old buildings also remain. This is the same St. Joseph Church founded by Hayti's early pioneers. Once again the church is the center of hope. The place of worship is prominent in the efforts of a community to unite towards a shared future.

---

[15] McCants, 51-52.

[16] McCants, 52-53.

[17] "Digitally Reconstructing Hayti," University of North Carolina, assessed December 5, 2017. http://mainstreet.lib.unc.edu/projects/durham/index.php/markers/view/144

There is also renewed interest in the leaders who helped build the community of Hayti. This heritage can inspire the efforts for community renewal. As we learn more about the people of Hayti's past, we will learn how people from oppressed spaces can liberate themselves by building communities of promise.

EATONVILLE, FLORIDA
MOSES BUILDS LEADERS

Build homes, and plan to stay. Plant gardens, and eat the food they produce. Jeremiah 29:5

In 1935, Alan Lomax, one of the most renowned musicologist and folklorist of the twentieth century travelled to Florida with scholars Zora Neale Hurston and Mary Elizabeth Barnicle to study the African American residents who lived there. On June 22, Lomax sat down to write a letter addressed to his family after collecting oral histories from the local residents. In his letter, he wrote about the distinctiveness of Eatonville as a Black town in that "the White people of this part of the country have left them to themselves pretty much for the last fifty years." Lomax's working relationship with Zora Neale Hurston, who grew up in Eatonville, surely helped him gain the local residents' trust.[1]

An Incorporated Town

Even today, Eatonville remains a curiosity. Although there were a number of Black towns and settlements throughout the United States in the years after Reconstruction, not all of them were incorporated. What makes an incorporated town distinct from an unincorporated town is that it is a municipality that has received its recognition from the state to elect its own town government. As an incorporated town, residents in Eatonville elected their own officers and selected their police without intrusion. As a people coming out of slavery and Reconstruction, the psychological impact and privilege of seeing African

---

[1] Alan Lomax, Letter to Family, June 22, 1935, Alan Lomax Collection, Manuscripts, Georgia, Florida, and the Bahamas, 1935 June-Aug. 1935. Manuscript/Mixed Material. Retrieved from the Library of Congress, https://www.loc.gov/item/afc2004004.ms120262/. (Accessed December 4, 2017.); Valerie Boyd, *Wrapped in rainbows: a biography of Zora Neal Hurston* (London: Virago, 2004), 322

Americans effectively manage their livelihoods instilled in Zora Neale Hurston and other residents the importance of Black independence and self-determination.

Eatonville and its neighbor sister city, Maitland, are connected by their joint histories. Before the Civil War, this region in central Florida remained relatively unsettled until the conclusion of the Indian Wars. Then settlers began to move to the area. There was need, however, for laborers to clear the roads and work in the orange groves. African Americans, seeking better opportunities in the post Reconstruction South, came as Hurston wrote:

> "Things were moving so swiftly that there was plenty to do, with good pay. Other Negroes in Georgia and West Florida heard of the boom in South Florida from Crescent City to Cocoa and they came. No more back-bending over rows of cotton; no more fear of the fury of the Reconstruction. Good pay, sympathetic White folks and cheap land, soft to the touch of a plow. Relatives and friends were sent for."[2]

As White men and women came to Maitland they built lavish homes on their large estates surrounding the lakes. African Americans settled in the less prosperous area around St. John's Hole. By 1884, enough people resided in the area that local residents decided to incorporate the town of Maitland. In her autobiography, Hurston wrote, "Maitland had grown big enough, and simmered down enough, to consider a formal city government."[3]

The story of Eatonville parallels the theme behind the passage in Exodus 18:21-24. There is a need for good leaders. Every healthy community needs leaders who are devoted to its success. In the passage, Moses with advice from his father-in-law, Jethro, picked faithful, honest, and capable men to be the leaders who helped the community flourish. In the same way, Eatonville wouldn't have become

---

[2] Zora Neale Hurston, *Dust Tracks on a Road: An Autobiography* (New York: HarperCollins, 2006), 5.
[3] Ibid.,

a haven and oasis for Blacks in Florida if it wasn't for the competent leadership that helped to build the town.

Because the town did not exclude African Americans from voting in the first local election, two Black men, Tony Taylor and Joe Clark, won the most important positions, sheriff and town marshal respectively. Although more research is necessary to understand what exactly happened after this, it seems that the men were allowed to assume their elected positions. Zora Neale Huston and her biographer, Valerie Boyd, both argue that the relations between the White and Black townspeople were good. However, Alan Lomax provides a slightly different and less positive version. Lomax writes that when the two Black men won the election the White people in the town "gently suggested that they better get their own town so they could run everything to suit themselves." Lomax continues that "two or three got together and gave the land, the Negroes largely moved out of Maitland (which is only a mile away) and settled down in their own little place with two Negro police and a Negro mayor to govern them." Both versions, are in agreement that prominent landowner, Lewis Lawrence, a White man from New York and Josiah Eaton (a local landowner) initiated conversations with Joe Clark and other African American leaders about the possibility of setting up their own town which would be different from Maitland. Eventually, Lawrence sold roughly 12 acres of land to Joe Clark who later subdivided the property. Clark sold that land in small parcels at a reasonable price to African Americans. This land, along with about 10 acres in the tract, which was the location of the Black Methodist church, formed the new town of Eatonville. Like many Black towns, the church was the first permanent structure. Later, this Methodist church would be renamed the Lawrence African Methodist Episcopal Church in recognition of Lewis Lawrence.[4]

However, it is not appropriate to say that White resistance to Black rule in Maitland served as the only incentive to establish an all-Black town. According to Hurston, Joe Clark, an African American settler in

---

[4] Allan Lomax Letter; Boyd, 21

Maitland, desperately wanted to establish a Black town which would provide Black people freedom from White intrusion. Hurston wrote:

> "Joe Clarke had asked himself, why not a Negro town? Few of the Negroes were interested. It was too vaulting for their comprehension. A pure Negro town! If nothing but their own kind was in it, who was going to run it? With no White folks to command them, how would they know what to do? Joe Clarke had plenty of confidence in himself to do the job, but few others could conceive of it."[5]

Zora Neale Hurston's Inspiration

Successful families, communities, and organizations leave an impression on the peoplethey contact. The Black family, for example, has traditionally served as a buffer against racism and oppression. Successful African Americans organizations, including our churches, have and continue to instill a sense of belonging to its members. I personally know the importance of community because my life experiences are but one example of the important role communities have on the individual. Growing up, I had the privilege to live in a small farming community in Virginia named Saluda. There I was surrounded by my parents, grandparents, and family members on the same land my ancestors had lived. Many years later, I still feel the impact of the small little church that provided my first public speaking opportunities and helped instruct me in the ways of the Lord. Indeed, the feel and rhythm of my home, the friendships, and the overall vibe of the town has left an indelible mark on my life. No matter how far I travel, Saluda and its people are still home. Unfortunately, very few people today enjoy the types of experiences I had growing up because these communities are no longer the norm. Today, far too many of us do not know our neighbors, the people we work with, or even the members of our churches. For Zora Neale Hurston, however, her experiences in Eatonville gave her that connection. Although Hurston was born in

---

[5] Hurston, *Dust Tracks*, 5-6

Alabama, it was her life in Eatonville that defined the rest of her life. In numerous books and reflections, Hurston claimed Eatonville as her home, even though she probably spent only ten years there. Hurston once referred to the town as "what you might call hitting a straight lick with a crooked stick." This was different from her statements about the area where she was born. Indeed Hurston wrote that her father had "been born near Notasulga, Alabama, in an outlying district of landless Negroes, and Whites not too much better off. It was 'over the creek,' which was just like saying on the wrong side of the railroad tracks." While Eatonville inspired Hurston with a feeling of determination, she had little positive to say about Notasulga.[6]

Eatonville's promise of an oasis from racism and the opportunity to establish a new life brought people to the town. Eatonville was a place Black people could come to and establish themselves. Hurston wrote about her parents in these terms, "So these two began their new life. Both of them swore that things were going to be better, and it came to pass as they said. They bought land, built a roomy house, planted their acres and reaped."[7]

Zora Neale Hurston's family thrived in Eatonville. Her father became a landowner, and was elected mayor twice. He also served as pastor of the Macedonia Baptist Church and his wife, Hurston's mother, was the superintendent of the Sunday School. Hurston's's memories extend beyond the church. She also noted her relationship with Joe Clark, the town's founder. Hurston wrote about the impact of his store:

> "Men sat around the store on boxes and benches and passed this world and the next one through their mouths. The right and the wrong, the who, when and why was passed on, and nobody doubted the conclusions. Women stood around there on Saturday nights and had it proven to the community that their husbands

---

[6] Hurston, *Dust Tracks*, 1; 7
[7] Hurston, *Dust Tracks*, 10

were good providers, put all of their money in their wives' hands and generally glorified them."[8]

People who are inspired by something always find ways to promote it. Eatonville served as a foundation for Zora Neale Hurston's prose and ideology. Indeed, in one of her last writings, a 1955 editorial to the *Orlando Sentinel*, Hurston, by that time an impoverished woman, was still devoted to Black self-governance. Her advocacy for Black independence seems to have driven her lack of enthusiasm for the Brown v. Board of Education decision:

> "It is well known that I have no sympathy nor respect for the 'tragedy of color' school of thought among us, whose fountainhead is the pressure group concerned in this court ruling. I can see no tragedy in being too dark to be invited to a White school social affair. The Supreme Court would have pleased me more if they had concerned themselves about enforcing the compulsory education provisions for Negroes in the South as is done for White children. The next 10 years would be better spent in appointing truant officers and looking after conditions in the homes from which the children come. Use to the limit what we already have."

The Past to the Future

Eatonville was always a small town. The fact that it was a small town meant that relationships between people had to be close. Most Black residents found work in Maitland or other surrounding areas. However, local residents did have gardens and farms which provided them with food. Nonetheless, outside of Joe Clark's store in the early years, very few businesses existed. There were skilled African Americans in the town such as John Hurston, who in addition to being a minister was also a carpenter. Eatonville also included a number of skilled professional women including Laura Clark and Sarah Taylor. Most residents, worked in farming or in the homes and restaurants of nearby Maitland. This is confirmed by Alan Lomax's observations when he

---

[8] Hurston, *Dust Tracks*, 41; 45

wrote that "most of the inhabitants (pop. 350) either work in the orange groves or in the kitchens of the rich White folks. . ."[9]

In addition to the church, the Robert T. Hungerford Industrial School was the other major institution in Eatonville. This school, which promoted the industrial education platform of Booker T. Washington, found tremendous support throughout the United States. Indeed, the school and Eatonville intrigued Booker T. Washington. As he did with other Black towns, Washington promoted African American self-determination and he was even one of the early donors to the industrial school. The founding of the school also traces back to a Maitland resident doctor named Dr. Robert T. Hungerford. Hungerford was one of the few people to help educate African Americans in Central Florida. Upon his death, his family donated land in the area to recent Tuskegee graduates Russell and Mary Calhoun so that they could establish a Black school. The Calhouns had recently moved to Eatonville and opened a home school for sewing. By 1889, with the help of the Hungerfords and other philanthropists, they opened the Hungerford Industrial School. The school not only educated students from Eatonville, but also throughout the entire region through 12th grade. Four years after opening, the school had more than 100 students, both male and female. Areas of specialization included trades from dressmaking to wheelwright (builder and repairer of wooden wheels). Students lived and worked on campus. The industrial school also enhanced the number of skilled professionals in Eatonville.[10]

Eatonville remains an example of Black leadership and self-governance. From Joe Clark and Zora Neale Hurston's father John Hurston, the leaders of the community were cut from the same cloth. They understood the value of discipline, hard work, and collective action. Their example is something to be mimicked much like the leadership

---

[9] Boyd, 14; *1900 U.S. Census, Eatonville, Orange, Florida*; Roll: *175*, Page *12B*. Enumeration District: *0117*, Family History Library Film, 1240175, *Laura Clark and Sarah Taylor, digital images*, (http://www.ancestry.com: *assessed December 7, 2017*); *Lomax Letter*,

[10] Russell C. Calhoun, "A Negro Community Builder," in *Tuskegee & its People: their ideals and achievements*, ed. Booker T. Washington and Emmett Scott (D. Appleton: Boston, 1906), 317-337.

selection of Moses in Exodus chapter 18. When our leaders have these qualities, our communities prosper, just like Eatonville and many other Black communities did.

Today Eatonville is experiencing a revival in the same wayits most well-known resident, Zora Neale Hurston, does. Although relatively forgotten after her death in 1960, by the 1980s, Hurston's work, particularly her best work, *Their Eyes Were Watching God*, has become a part of America's literary canon. Now it is taught in schools throughout the nation. Many of the same issues that continue to plague Eatonville throughout its existence. This includes a high poverty level that remains twice the national level. However, this fact is reflective of realities across our nation as the African American unemployment is roughly twice the rate of White Americans. Nonetheless, the spirit of Black self-governance and progress in Eatonville residents remains. For example, in 1989 the townspeople, in a response to a proposed road that would have divided the town, protested by organizing a Zora Neale Hurston Festival. People came from everywhere and the county backed down on the road. Each year, people return to Eatonville for the Zora Neale Hurston Festival. The town remains a curiosity but its residents continue to see the value in their community that Zora saw. They stand on the foundational pillars of Eatonville: the church, the school, and the family.

JACKSON WARD
BUILDING WITHIN BOUNDARIES

See, I have taught you decrees and laws as the LORD my God commanded me, so that you may follow them in the land you are entering to take possession of it. (Deuteronomy 4:5)

In many ways, African American history is analogous to the Israelite sojourn to the Promised Land. In both cases, prejudice kept the communities from many things. Yet even within the restraints, God provided ways for his people to build a community. This is also the case with Jackson Ward. Jackson Ward wasn't created by African Americans; it was a political construct from the Reconstruction period when the city council in Richmond, Virginia gerrymandered the northern portions of the city into a super majority Black district. In creating this majority district of African Americans, the conservatives on Richmond's city council gave Blacks control over one district while blocking them from control over the other five districts. Nonetheless, God continued to bless his community.[1]

Brook Avenue to Jackson Ward

Jackson Ward was more than simply a political conspiracy to suppress Black votes. The established district didn't restrict Black participation in social or business endeavors. People like Maggie Lena Walker, who lived in Jackson Ward, bypassed other churches in the ward to attend

---

[1] Michael Chesson, "Richmond's Black Councilmen, 1871-1896" in *Southern Black Leaders of the Reconstruction Era* edited by Howard Rabinowitz (Chicago: University of Illinois Press, 1982) pp. 191-222

the First Baptist Church a few miles away. Other Blacks who lived right outside Jackson Ward conducted their business in the ward.[2]

African Americans had lived in the Jackson Ward area long before Richmond's city council created the district. In the early nineteenth century, a concentration of prominent landowning free African Americans lived around Brook Avenue in part of what would become Jackson Ward. Benjamin Wythe Judah, a free African American, inherited a lot on Brook Avenue from Isaac Judah, a Jewish rabbi who had raised him and his brother. Within two years, David Judah, Isaac Judah's nephew and estate executor, began to sell other lots on Brook Avenue to African Americans. Benjamin Judah purchased another two lots from Isaac Judah. Other free African Americans soon purchased lots also, including Henry Bradley, John Adams, and Mahala Bassinett.[3]

Coming together to establish community

Black Richmonders have a long history of helping each other through their involvement in self-help organizations. Historically, these associations allowed them to establish a larger base of capital, which not only bolstered their real and personal estates, but also helped them provide intellectual and social capital to those who needed it. The most important example of these organizations in the antebellum period was the Burying Society of the Free People of Color established in the 1830s. The society not only provided a burial ground for free African Americans, but it also gave elite Blacks the opportunity to come together on a regular basis.[4]

---

[2] M.M. Branch, "Maggie Lena Walker," The Encyclopedia of Virginia, www. EncyclopediaVirginia.org/Maggie_Lena_Walker_1864-1934 (assessed December 7, 2017)

[3] *Richmond City Will Book 4* p. 361, Library of Virginia; *Richmond City Deed Book 30* pp. 51; 54, Library of Virginia; *Richmond City Deed Book 49*, pp. 528-529, Library of Virginia; *Richmond City Deed Book 49*, pp. 529-530, Library of Virginia; *Richmond City Deed Book 51*, pp. 131; 271; *Richmond City Personal Property Tax Book*, 1855; Library of Virginia; *Richmond City Deed Book 52* pp. 345; 347; 351; 355; 366; *Richmond City Deed Book 53*, p. 271, Library of Virginia; *Richmond City Deed Book 54*, pp. 96; 298, Library of Virginia

[4] Carey H. Latimore, *The Role of Southern Free Blacks During the Civil War Era: The Life of Free African Americans in Richmond, Virginia 1850-1876* (Lewistown: Edwin Mellen Press, 2015), 60-63.

After the Civil War, Richmond became a center of military activity. The Freedmen's Bureau, a bureau charged with helping people negatively affected by the Civil War, had a strong presence in the city. The bureau had its greatest success establishing Black schools in Richmond. One of the first schools established in the Jackson Ward area by the Freedmen's Bureau was the Richmond Normal and High School. These schools provided opportunities for all Black Richmonders. The school had a liberal arts and vocational curriculum and was intended to promote Black prosperity in a variety of occupations.[5]

Even before the war, many African Americans had some ability to read and write. A few weeks after the war's conclusion, one local petition wrote that "the law of Slavery severely punished those who taught us to read and write, but, notwithstanding this, 3,000 of us can read, and at least 2,000 can read and write, and a large number of us are engaged in useful and profitable employment."

Even though the bureau schools did a tremendous job, they were not the only source of education. In 1866, the editor of the *London Athenaeum* traveled through Richmond's black community and saw up to 40 places that educated black people "mostly in garrets or down in vaults; poor rooms with scant supplies of benches, desks, and books." These underground schools almost certainly existed in prewar years.[6]

It didn't take long for Richmond to have institutions dedicated to college training for Black students. With the help of northern philanthropists, local African Americans helped form the Richmond Theological Seminary, a male-only institution. It took a number of years for Black women in Richmond to have a similar institution of higher learning. In 1883, the Hartshorn Memorial College opened and provided women with teacher training and vocational instruction.[7]

---

[5] Elsa Barkley Brown *Uncle Ned's Children: Negotiating Community and Freedom in Post Emancipation Richmond, Virginia.* 1994, 78-9

[6] *New York Tribune*, June 17, 1865; Letter from Committee of Richmond Blacks in The Papers of Andrew Johnson edited by LeRoy P. Graf (Knoxville: University of Tennessee Press, 1967) pp.210-213. as referenced in Brown, 79

[7] Brown, 103-111.

Throughout the late nineteenth century, the majority of teachers for Black students were White. For example, in 1880, Elsa Barkley Brown wrote that there were only eleven "Black teachers in the public schools, all at Navy Hill (Jackson ward)."

Black Richmonders eventually demanded Black teachers for their children and they formed organizations such as the Virginia Educational and Historical Association to push for them. By the dawn of the twentieth century even many instructors at the seminary and at Hartshorn, including Rosa K. Jones, a community leader and music teacher, were African American. The transition to Black instruction would be completed by the early twentieth century.[8]

Politics within boundaries

The growing power of the Republican Party in Richmond during Reconstruction meant that local Blacks had a vehicle to organize around. By 1867, two men, Joseph Cox and Lewis Lindsay emerged as the most important Black political leaders in Richmond. Both men proved to be effective grassroots organizers. Born free, Cox had been a day laborer before the war. After the war, he owned a small store and later became the leader of the Political Aid Society. Cox also worked at the Richmond Customs House, a local Republican organization that provided jobs to Republican Party supporters.[9]

The tide changed, however, in 1870 when Reconstruction ended in Virginia. The gains of the previous years couldn't be replicated without federal support. In Richmond, however, the transition didn't completely disenfranchise African Americans. Because of the creation of Jackson Ward, African Americans did gain control over the common council seats of that district as well as its seats on the city's board of aldermen. A majority of the people who represented Jackson Ward

---

[8] Brown 95 and 98-99; *Richmond Planet*, July 20, 1901.
[9] Latimore, 154-155

came from the prominent classes such as Joseph Farrar, John Adams, and Richard Forrester.[10]

The decline of the Readjuster Party in the mid 1880s, however, and the ascendency of the more conservative Democratic Party led to fewer political opportunities for Blacks. Their political potential was restricted. And, it continued to erode after the 1902 Virginia constitutional convention which implemented poll taxes and provided the Virginia General Assembly with the power to select local officials.

Economics within boundaries

Even though Black Richmonders found themselves limited from the larger political arena, Blacks who lived in Jackson Ward and its immediate outskirts continued to prosper economically and socially. Through networks of communication and association, Black Richmonders pooled their resources in their attempt to create a sustainable community.

The life of John Adams is a perfect example. Adams, a skilled plasterer and home builder, represented a new type of Black economic leader. Unlike most antebellum free Blacks who catered their businesses to the White elite, Adams had built houses for African Americans on credit and apparently garnered tremendous respect. He capitalized on these ties in the postwar period. As a result of his business savvy, his business boomed between 1865 and 1873. By 1873, he owned eleven lots in Richmond and rented most of them out. He also had connections to free African Americans in Petersburg.[11]

Part of Adams' success can be attributed to his connections with Brook Avenue's free African American community. For example, his children employed Joseph Farrar, a local carpenter. Farrar was the son-in-law of George Gray, a prominent prewar barber. Adams also rented many of his properties to former free Blacks. Although the prewar ties

---

[10] Chesson, 191-222. Also see Latimore, *Role of Southern Free Blacks.*
[11] Latimore, 171-173.

to Black leaders like Joseph Farrar and Benjamin Vandervall, who both became city councilman provided certain advantages, as the Jackson Ward community developed, prewar status wasn't a barrier for Blacks with less privileged backgrounds. Success depended on how Black people were able to cater to the Black community. The people who prospered in postwar Richmond did so not because of their prewar status, but because of their ability to transition. While prewar status and prosperity depended on catering services to a White clientele, postwar prominence depended to catering services to the Black community.

Uniting to build a community

Many Black Richmonders did very well individually in their businesses and together, they demonstrated a desire to give back to their community through their churches and fraternal organizations. Black Richmonders took pride in these organizations and worked hard through them to provide opportunity for other residents. Black church leaders played a central role in bringing the community together. Although the background of the ministers who led these congregations differed, they all shared a dedication to promoting education in their communities through the church. The most prominent men and women in Jackson Ward belonged to a church and they weren't ashamed to let everyone know. The *Richmond Planet*, the Black newspaper of Richmond, consistently profiled prominent Black residents, never failing to inform the readers of their memberships in churches and fraternal organizations.

Black ministers and church leaders, particularly those in Jackson Ward, held tremendous influence in the community. Not only did the pastors represent their congregations, but these church leaders often held prominent positions in self-help societies and were also members of local lodges and fraternal organizations such as the Knights of Pythias and the Order of Calanthe. The Knights of Pythias united prominent Black men many of whom were either pastors or men who had strong business interests. John Mitchell, the Grand Chancellor of Virginia's Pythians, was ,the editor of the *Richmond Planet*. In 1901, he founded the Mechanics Savings Bank. The bank was located in the same building that the Pythians met. [12]

The pastor of Fifth Street Baptist Church, Dr. W.F. Graham, was also the president of an insurance company, the Richmond Beneficial Insurance Company. Additionally, he was a member of the Odd Fellows, another fraternal organization with a strong presence in Richmond. Amember on Graham's insurance companyboard was S.J. Gilpin, a shoe dealer. Gilpin was also a member of the Knights of the Pythias and the Order of St. Luke's. All of the ten directors belonged to a church in Richmond. This company also included women. In 1898, Mary E. Robinson was hired as the bank clerk.[13]

The Grand Fountain of the United Order of True Reformers operated the largest Black bank in Richmond. Originally a temperance society, by the late nineteenth century, the society entered into the insurance business. All of the leaders of the organization were members of a local church. By 1889, the True Reformer's Savings Bank was opened and had more than 10,000 depositors. In addition to insurance and the bank, the organization sold real estate and operated a store and a grocery.[14]

Black women also boldly established themselves in Jackson Ward. In 1897, a group of African American women in Jackson Ward, including Louisa Williams and Kate Holmes, formed the Women's Corner Stone Beneficial Association. Louisa Williams also organized the Knights and Ladies of Honor in 1897. These organizations, along with Richmond's Women's League and the Women's Union of the Independent Order of St. Luke's, provided leadership opportunities to Black women. The women who joined these organizations often participated in numerous charity endeavors throughout the entire city.[15]

---

[12] *Richmond Planet*, July 22, 1922.

[13] "Richmond Beneficial Insurance Company," *Richmond Planet*, January 4, 1902; "The Mechanics Savings Bank of Richmond, Virginia," *Richmond Planet*, January 6, 1906.

[14] Brown, 141.

[15] *Richmond Planet*, March 12, 1904.

These organizations provided the start for some of the most prominent Black women. The Independent Order of St. Luke's was one of the few organizations not specifically for women that provided them with leadership opportunities. In 1898, Rosa K. Jones was its president. Jones was one of the first Black female professors at Hartshorn College. She also had her own music school. Her vice president, Maggie Lena Walker, eventually becamehead of the entire organization. The young Walker had once delivered laundry to prominent White customers.

Walker had graduated from Richmond Normal and High School in 1883. As an educated woman, she took part in the emerging economic prosperity and community in Richmond. She joined other women in founding "the Woman's Union insurance business." In 1903, she helped found the St. Luke Penny Savings Bank and became its first president."[16]

The Order of the Calanthe, a fraternal organization for Black women, was the sister organization to the Knights of the Pythias. Like the Knights, the Calanthe provided funeral assistance to all its members. It also provided insurance to sick members. The Calanthe also had a children's department called the Bands of Calanthe. This organization brought young kids together, often meeting regularly at the Pythian hall. They also organized picnics for kids.

One of the most active women in the Calanthe was Clara Pervall. Pervall involved herself in numerous community organizations such as the Auxiliary of the Negro Hospital and the YWCA. Pervall, a registered nurse, proved herself as an able fundraiser and leader, helping to establish a YWCA for young Black women.[17]

---

[16] Brown, 130-131.

[17] *Richmond Planet*, Feb, 8, 1908; *Richmond Planet*, Sept 6, 1902; *Richmond Planet*, June 20, 1908; *Richmond Planet*, Nov 4, 1922

Decline and Renewal

By 1920 Black Richmonders in Jackson Ward had created a community that provided almost every service and occupation that could be expected. The district also served as a local hot spot for the most prominent Black entertainers. Real estate agencies sold properties. The churches and fraternal organizations provided entertainment for youth. Indeed, several large athletic clubs helped mentor young Black Richmonders. There was a very strong YMCA and YWCA. Richmond even had a Black art gallery.

The challenges for Jackson Ward, however, emerged around the same time as World War I. In a similar trajectory to Mound Bayou, the community suffered tremendous population losses as Black residents moved north.

The *Richmond Planet* certainly recognized the possibility of population decline in 1918 when it began printing stories about the migration in a more negative light. In one article it stated that "the high cost of living" nullifies the decent salaries offered in the north. Another piece reported that "in the north the colored citizen is being regarded as an interloper and outside of the pale of law."

Even though the editors of the *Richmond Planet* were careful to not openly criticize the migration, they certainly seem to have been concerned about the potential implications of such migration. Nevertheless, the migration would continue, and increased even more during the Depression and World War II.

This continued when an interstate highway split the community. Homeownership dropped and tenancy increased as Black people moved outside the traditional Black neighborhoods into the suburbs by the late twentieth century.[18]

---

[18] *Richmond Planet*, Jan 5, 1918

The boundaries that once kept Black Richmonders confined to one area of the city didn't remain. At the same time, not staying within the old boundaries caused the community to decline.

Jackson Ward has yet to regain its once privileged status. Still, it is going through a renaissance. It is now a National Historic District and today one can find in it museums, art spaces, and historical landmarks dedicated to the African American experience. Jackson Ward is alive once more.

FREEDMEN'S VILLAGE, ARLINGTON, VIRGINIA
JOSHUA'S BUILDING BLOCKS

4 So Joshua called together the twelve men he had appointed from the Israelites, one from each tribe, 5 and said to them, "Go over before the ark of the Lord your God into the middle of the Jordan. Each of you is to take up a stone on his shoulder, according to the number of the tribes of the Israelites, 6 to serve as a sign among you. In the future, when your children ask you, 'What do these stones mean?' 7 tell them that the flow of the Jordan was cut off before the ark of the covenant of the Lord. When it crossed the Jordan, the waters of the Jordan were cut off. These stones are to be a memorial to the people of Israel forever." (Joshua 4:4-7)

One of the most important aspects of the Civil War and emancipation is the variety of ways African Americans pursued their freedom. African American liberation extended far beyond the Emancipation Proclamation and Juneteenth. Even before either of those proclamations, many slaves simply packed up what they had and abandoned the plantations and farms where they hadlived . For example, when Union Major-General Benjamin Butler and his army seized control of Fort Monroe in Hampton, Virginia in August 1861, it set off a series of events that had tremendous ramifications for the future direction of emancipation and Reconstruction. Slaves from the nearby farms and plantations escaped from their masters seeking refuge at Fort Monroe. The slaves' actions forced General Butler to make a choice. He could send the slaves back to their masters, he could emancipate them (a risky move since President Lincoln opposed such measures), or find a compromise position. Butler chose a compromise position by declaring the slaves at Fort Monroe contrabands of war. This decision allowed the contrabands to stay at the fort. While Butler didn't address the slaves' legal status, his declaration did give him the authority to force the contrabands to work at the fort. Butler's offer was not perfect, but it was for many slaves a much better alternative than returning to their masters. Hundreds perhaps thousands of African Americans followed the initial contrabands into Fort Monroe.

As a child, I heard stories about my great-great grandfather, William Harris, was one of the slaves who escaped from his master and presented himself to the Union Army at Fort Monroe. My ancestor kept his legacy alive as a memorial for future generations. The brave actions of men and women like my great-great grandfather helped force the federal government to clarify the status of slaves that came under the care of the union army.

Stories like my great-great grandfather's and the story of the men and women of Freedmen's Village are like the twelve stones Joshua commanded the Israelites to place on top of one another as a memorial. They remind us of where we have come. They are part of the history that we are still living today. It is important to continue to rehearse these stories as they bind us together as a community.

In 1861 and 1862, Congress passed the First and Second Confiscation Acts. The First Confiscation Act in 1861, stated that the Union Army had the authority to confiscate property (i.e., including slaves) from Confederates. The Second Confiscation Act in 1862, provided a way for confiscated slaves to be freed, in sense a precursor to the Emancipation Proclamation. On the ground, however, the First and Second Confiscation acts were difficult to implement. Ultimately, many Blacks who came to Union lines seeking refuge didn't have their status determined.

Throughout the war, military authorities in the Washington D.C., metropolitan area struggled to find a solution for the overcrowding in the contraband camps. The fact that the metropolitan area included two states and a district with different laws regarding slavery added to the dilemma. In 1862, Washington D.C., abolished the institution of slavery.

Maryland, even though it remained a part of the Union, didn't abolish slavery until November, 1864. Slaves, understanding this, and perhaps fearful of their masters selling them even further south, sought refuge in Washington D.C near Union encampments. Although the Union erected camps for the refugees, the sheer influx of contrabands, along with poor management in the camps led to horrific conditions including disease and death. A report from one of the hastily-erected camps stated that "in all the wretchedness and poverty incident to their former condition as chattels, hungry and in rags, their whole appearance piteously appealing for succor." At Camp Barker, one contraband camp in the capital, the death rate was roughly 25 former slaves a week.[1]

Just as General Butler did at Fort Monroe, the War Department in Washington D.C, forced thousands of contrabands to work. Some of the jobs Blacks did for the War Department included working at the forts, building fortifications, and constructing roads. The War Department compensated the former slaves with equal pay as White employees, but in Washington D.C., former slaves had to pay a contraband tax.

Establishing a Legacy Freedmen's Village

The American Missionary Association and the Freedmen's Relief Association, two organizations that wanted to help African Americans, worked with the War Department to set up a contraband village outside the capital. Because these organizations viewed the military camps in Washington D.C., as a humanitarian crisis, they believed that establishing a village outside the crowded capital would make life better for the newly freed African American. At the same time, the twoorganizations believed that a camp away from the capital would make it easier for them to help educate and evangelize the African Americans.

---

[1] *New York Times*, May 3, 1862; Reidy, Joseph P. ""Coming from the Shadow of the Past": The Transition from Slavery to Freedom at Freedmen's Village, 1863-1900." *The Virginia Magazine of History and Biography* 95, no. 4 (1987): 403-28. http://www.jstor.org/stable/4248971.

All they needed to set up a community was a location, and unfortuationly, a suitable location was already under Union control. In 1861, the Union Army had seized the property of General Robert E. Lee and his wife, Martha Custis Lee. Located right across the Potomac River in Arlington, Virginia, it was a perfect location to move the former slaves. By the summer of 1863, the military had constructed the village and started transferring Black people there. In December of that same year, the military sponsored a celebration to dedicate Freedmen's Village. Many White residents in Arlington County, however, didn't approve of the resettlement project. An editorial in the *Arlington Gazette* openly questioned the value of moving contrabands to Freedman's village and hoped that "surplus stock [contrabands at Freedmen's Village] were moved in the same direction [they came from]." Nonetheless, within a year, the village consisted of roughly fifty duplex homes that accommodated two families each.[2]

There was much more to Freedmen's Village than just residential homes. Unlike the military camps, the creators of the village wanted it to be more like a community. They constructed a hospital, church, and industrial school. Mount Zion Baptist, the first of three Black churches in Freedmen's Village served as the pillar of the community. Mount Zion was the most important and visible institution in the village and it not only attended to the spiritual and educational needs of the community, but it also was the location of numerous town meetings and political conventions. For the first decade of its existence, the church was led by Reverend Robert S. Laws, a leader and educator in the community. An educated African American minister, Laws was affiliated with the American Missionary Association and worked as one of the first educators in Freedmen's Village.[3]

---

[2] "From the Washington Chronicle." *The Arlington Gazette*, July 14, 1864. From the Library of Congress Website Chronicling America: Historic American Newspapers, https://chroniclingamerica.loc.gov/lccn/sn85025007/1864-07-14/ed-1/seq-2. "Local News" *Evening Star*, Dec. 2, 1863

[3] "South Washington News." *The Washington Bee*, January 11, 1890. From the Library of Congress Website Chronicling America: Historic American Newspapers, http://chroniclingamerica.loc.gov/lccn/sn84025891/1890-01-11/ed-1/seq-3/

During the period that the Freedmen's Bureau and the military oversaw the village, residents had to work for the military or find employment nearby. Residents could be forcibly transferred to and from Freedmen's Village. Some residents deemed too old or unable to work were moved to Mason's Island near Georgetown in the District of Columbia[4]

During the years of military rule and Freedmen's Bureau control (1863-1870), residents enjoyed few freedoms in Freedmen's Village. Another problem for the residents was that the plots of land were too small for them to farm for profit. This problem got worse by generation because each generation had less land than the previous. Another problem was that the Freedmen's Bureau also required residents to pay rent. The discontent over rent was such a problem that Rev. Laws, united residents in the village to protest the treatment.[5]

The Past Provides a View to a Future

The fact that Freedmen's Village sat on Robert E. Lee's plantation made it a center of attention. At the same time, even more important, was the fact that the experiment at Freedmen's Village could have broader implications for the south after the war. Sojourner Truth, the famed Black abolitionist, visited the village in 1864 and stayed for six months. Truth was a member of the Freedman's Relief Association and worked at Freedman's Village. Her organization wanted to help the residents by providing them with moral and religious instruction.[6]

The population at the village included not only former contrabands but also free African Americans and former slaves from Arlington House, the name of the Custis/Lee plantation. The African Americans connected to the Custis plantation had more education and skills than other residents at Freedmen's Village. Of all of the residents living in Freedmen's Village, no family held more influence than the Syphax

---

[4] Reidy, 411; "Affairs in Georgetown." The *Evening Star*, May 8, 1865. From the Library of Congress Website Chronicling America: Historic American Newspapers, http://chroniclingamerica.loc.gov/lccn/sn83045462/1865-05-08/ed-1/seq-2/

[5] Reidy, 419-422

[6] *New York Times*, May 3, 1862

family. The Syphax family had accompanied the Custis family when they moved to Arlington House from George Washington's plantation at Mount Vernon. The family head, Charles Syphax, was a house servant in George Custis' home. The son of a free Black father and enslaved mother on the Custis plantation, his mother's status meant that he was a slave. During the Civil War, Syphax entertained the soldiers with his personal recollections of American leaders including George Washington, Thomas Jefferson , and James Monroe. Syphax married Maria Carter, the African American daughter of the slavemaster George Custis. George Custis eventually freed his mistress, daughter, and grandchildren. Even though he didn't free Charles Syphax, heave he family some land on the plantation.[7]

By 1860, the free Syphax family members in Arlington included Maria Syphax, her mother, and four other Syphax family members. By that year, some of the Syphax children had moved to Washington D.C., probably in search of better work and educational opportunities. By this time, Washington, D.C. had a thriving free Black community. Maria's eldest son, William, had livedbetween Washington, D.C., and Virginia, and was educated in private schools in the capital. By 1870, William Syphax was one of the wealthiest Black men in Washington D.C., owning more than $21,000 in real estate and working as a porter/messenger. William Syphax also became a prominent leader of Black education in the area and was first treasurer of the Board of trustees of the Colored Public Schools of Washington, D.C.. He also was employed as a copyist and messenger for the Interior Department.[8]

As free Black and contraband communities came together at Freedmen's Village, the Syphax family helped to ease the transition from slavery to

---

[7] Preston, E. Delorus. "William Syphax, a Pioneer in Negro Education in the District of Columbia." *The Journal of Negro History* 20, no. 4 (1935): 449. doi:10.2307/2714262; "The Syphax Family," *National Park Service, NPS.GOV, last modified*, Apr. 11, 2017. https://www.nps.gov/arho/learn/historyculture/syphax.htm.

[8] 1860 U.S. Census, *Alexandria, Virginia*, Roll: *M653_1331*, Page: *942*. Family History Library Film, *805331*, Maria Syphax, digital image, (http://Ancestry.com: assessed December 7, 2017); 1870 U.S. Census, Washington Ward 1, Washington, District of Columbia; Roll: *M593_123*, Page: *3A*, Family History Library Film: *545622*, William Syphax, digital image, (http://ancestry.com: assessed December 7, 2017; Evelyn Reid Syphax "William Syphax: Community Leader" *Arlington Historical Society,* The American Journal of Education, Volume 19, 244-5.

freedom for the entire community. Ellen Reeves, the oldest daughter of Charles and Maria Syphax was one of the first teachers at the AMA school in Freedmen's Village. At the school, she directed sewing. John and Austin Syphax, other sons of Charles and Maria Syphax, became political leaders in Freedmen's Village. While little is known about their early life, both probably had a similar upbringing to elder brother, William. Austin Syphax appears by 1868 as part of a convention to nominate delegates for the Congressional Convention. In 1870, he had been elected Superintendent of the Poor. Although his brother, John, does not appear in the enumeration of Freedmen'sVillage in 1865, by 1872, he lived in Freedmen's Village and was also active in Republican Party politics. In that year, county residents selected both brothers to serve as county delegates for the Republican Party. Austin would later become a justice of the peace for Arlington. In 1874, Arlington residents elected John Syphax (the first African American to serve in the House of Delegates) as a representative for Arlington to the House of Delegates and he served one term. After his term ended, he served Alexandria from 1875 to 1879 as a treasurer.[9]

Other former slaves from the Arlington House prospered in the years after the Civil War. One other important family at Freedmen's Village was the Gray family. Headed by Thornton and Selina Gray, they were freed by Robert E. Lee, who was the executor of his father- in-law's estate. Once free, Thornton Gray acquired land and farmed it. In 1870,

---

[9] "History of Schools for the Colored Population," *The American Journal of Education* edited by Henry Barnard vol. 3 (Hartford: CT, 1870), 245, digital copy, (https://books.google.com/books?id=UYoXAtBf00sC&pg=PA245&dq=ellen+reeves+syphax+arlington&hl=en&sa=X&ved=0ahUKEwjfvPeD6frXAhXKLSYKHWofBpMQ6AEILDAB#v=onepage&q=ellen%20reeves%20syphax%20arlington&f=false: assessed December 7, 2017); Syphax, "Community Leader;" "Radical county Convention," Alexandria Gazette, May 25, 1858. From the Library of Congress website Chronicling America: Historic American Newspapers, https://chroniclingamerica.loc.gov/lccn/sn85025007/1868-05-25/ed-1/seq-3/#date1=1789&index=0&rows=20&words=Austin+Syphax&searchType=basic&sequence=0&state=&date2=1943&proxtext=Austin+Syphax&y=15&x=10&dateFilterType=yearRange&page=1." "County Radicals," Alexandria Gazette, October 25, 1872, From the Library of Congress website Chronicling America: Historic American Newspapers, https://chroniclingamerica.loc.gov/lccn/sn85025007/1872-10-25/ed-1/seq-3/#date1=1789&index=1&rows=20&words=Austin+Syphax&searchType=basic&sequence=0&state=&date2=1943&proxtext=Austin+Syphax&y=15&x=10&dateFilterType=yearRange&page=1. "Local News," Alexandria Gazette, June 28, 1875, From the Library of Congress Website Chronicling America: Historic American Newspapers, https://chroniclingamerica.loc.gov/lccn/sn85025007/1875-06-28/ed-1/seq-3/#date1=1789&index=12&rows=20&words=Austin+Syphax&searchType=basic&sequence=0&state=&date2=1943&proxtext=Austin+Syphax&y=15&x=10&dateFilterType=yearRange&page=1.

he was one of the few Blacks in Arlington who owned land. Almost forty years later, Gray remained a farmer on his small Arlington estate. Ada Gray, his daughter, was a local educator for many years.[10]

Fighting To Keep The Stones

During the less than forty years of Freedmen's Village's existence, Black residents had to consistently fight for their right to stay there. For the Syphax family, troubles began even before the war because George Custis never legally titled the property to his daughter, Maria Syphax. When the government seized the property during the war, it included the plot that the Syphax family had occupied for the last forty years and claimed as their own. Fortunately for the family, William Syphax used his connections in the House and Senate in 1866 to successfully push a bill through both chambers that permitted the land to be titled to his mother.[11]

In 1868, the Freedmen's Bureau tried to sell all the buildings at the village but a group of Black leaders helped to postpone the decision. Even though plans to sell the plantation proved unsuccessful, the Freedmen's Bureau did change the mode of operations at the village. The bureau moved the residents of the hospital and home for the poor to Washington, D.C., The remaining residents had to purchase the houses where they lived in and rent the land on which the houses stood. When the Freedmen's Bureau transferred the control to the post commander at Fort Whipple in 1870, the leases no longer existed.[12]

The next major challenge to the village came from the Custis family. In 1873, after the death of his parents, George Custis Lee, sued to reacquire his parents' plantation. Lee wanted to develop the property

---

[10] Black Heritage Museum of Arlington County, *Freedman's Village: Arlington's First Free Neighborhood* (Arlington, VA: Black Heritage Museum of Arlington County, 2002), 7; 1900 U.S. Census, *Arlington, Alexandria, Virginia*; Roll: *1698*; Page: *1B*, Enumeration District: *0001* Family History Library Film, microfilm *1241698*, *Thornton Gray, digital image,* (http://www.ancestry.com: *assessed December 7, 2017)*

[11] Preston, 455.

[12] Preston, 423-4; Anthony J. Gaughan, *The Last Battle of the Civil War: United States versus Lee, 1861-1883* (Baton Rouge: LSU Press, 2011), 75-76.

and remove all of the residents. Although successful in his attempt to acquire the plantation, before he could remove the residents, he arranged to sell the land back to the government. This allowed for Arlington Cemetery to remain in government hand and once again stalled the removal of the African Americans from Freedmen's Village.[13]

Money and the village's prime location, made the removal of the settlers ultimately unavoidable. Developers wanted access to the land near the cemetery. In 1887, the residents were told to leave. Again, they united to protest the move and John Syphax led the protests. Syphax argued that the settlers had been led to believe that they would gain access to the property. He asked why the government had encouraged African Americans to build structures including churches at their expense if the ultimate goal was to remove them.[14]

The protests of community residents made little difference. The sheer number of complaints about the community increased substantially in the late 1870s. Local newspapers consistently reported on the squalid conditions of the village and their belief that the community was crime-ridden. In addition, White residents considered the presence of the community to be disrespectful to the soldiers buried at Arlington. The *Washington Post* wrote that "the darkies made their homes there during the war and have been allowed to remain ever since, but, owing to their depredations on the timber on the reservation and in Arlington Cemetery, the Secretary of War has issued an order requiring all persons living within the limits of the reservation to move within thirty days."[15]

There was another reason White residents wanted to destroy the community--the small community held tremendous political influence. A *Washington Post* editorial wrote that "The presence of

---

13 Gaughan, 75-76.

[14] Robert M. Poole, On Hallowed Ground: The Story of Arlington National Cemetery (New York: Bloomsbury Press, 2010), 97-98.

[15] "The Arlington Taxes" in Alexandria Gazette, January 18, 1884, From the Library of Congress website Chronicling America: Historic American Newspapers, https://chroniclingamerica.loc.gov/lccn/sn85025007/1884-01-18/ed-1/seq-2/#date1=1875&index=1&rows=20&words=Freedmen+Village&searchType=basic&sequence=0&state=Virginia&date2=1885&proxtext=Freedmen%27s+village&y=6&x=18&dateFilterType=yearRange&page=1; "Freedman's Village Abolished" The Washington Post, Dec. 06, 1887

the negroes on the reservation has had a curious effect on the politics of Alexandria County. Numbering between 300 to 400 they have virtually controlled the county, electing, until very recently, their County Clerk, Commonwealth's Attorney, Overseer of the Poor and Board of Supervisors." One wonders if the African American community at Freedmen's Village hadn't become a successful community politically and socially if the protests against it would have been as loud.[16]

Memorials for the Future

The last residents left Freedmen's Village in 1900 and nothing remains of it today. Most of the members of the Syphax family left the area, including John Syphax, the longtime advocate for the community. Nevertheless, the "stones" the legacy of the community and the people who created and lived in Freedmen's Village remains. They remain at Arlington House, the old plantation house. The museum there and the grounds stand not only as a memorial to the war and all the members and persons connected with one of the south's most famous families, but it also stands as a testament to the lives lived, lost, and forgotten by history in Freedmen's Village.

---

[16] "Local Intelligence," The Washington Post, December, 7, 1887.

TUSKEGEE, ALABAMA
RAHAB HELPS TO BUILD

"Our future is before us, not behind us. We are a new race in a comparatively new country. Let any who may be included toward pessimism or discord consider with me for a few moments the opportunities that are before us. It is always of more value to consider our advantages rather than disadvantages."[1]

On the night of August 18, 1915, Booker T. Washington, perhaps the most famous black man in America, stood before the Negro National Business League and delivered the last speech of his life. Suffering from hypertension and overwork, Washington's speech examines the last half century of African American progress. Born a slave in 1856 in Virginia, Washington had few advantages of birth. A self-made man, who had labored in West Virginia's coal mines, he accomplished more than he could have ever dreamed of as a kid working in the dirty and polluted coal mines. Nonetheless, it was the coal mines that inspired him to dream. According to him, one day he heard the other miners talking about Hampton Institute. He wrote that "although I had no idea where it was, or how many miles away, or how I was going to reach it; I remembered only that I was on fire constantly with one ambition, and that was to go to Hampton. This thought was with me day and night." When reading his last speech you can feel his pride in the progress of the black community over the previous half century.[2]

While at Hampton, Washington learned the skills of diplomacy. Washington also developed a close friendship with Hampton's

---

[1] Booker T. Washington, "An Address Before the Negro National Business League," in *African American political thought, 1890-1930: Washington, Du Bois, Garvey, and Randolph.* Edited by Cary D. Wintz (New York, NY: Routledge, 2015), 73-78.

[2] Booker T. Washington, *Up from Slavery: An Autobiography* (Doubleday: Page & Company, 1907), 43.

founder and President, Samuel Chapman Armstrong, a former Union Army general. The two men's association lasted for the remainder of Armstrong's life. Indeed, throughout his life, Washington used his skills of diplomacy to cultivate important relationships with prominent white philanthropists, businessmen, and political leaders.

Tuskegee before Washington

Before the founding of Tuskegee Institute, Creek Indians inhabited Macon County, where the town of Tuskegee is located. Persuaded by white slave owners and other yeoman farmers, the United States government pushed local Creeks to evacuate the land. This led to the Second Creek War, a conflict between the Creek Indians and the United States Government. The end of this war provided an excuse for forcing the Creeks in Alabama to leave. Many of the white settlers who came in after the Creeks brought their slaves with them.[3]

Emancipation brought new challenges to African Americans. As a state, Alabama had a very small free black population before the Civil War. Therefore, almost all blacks in Alabama started their new lives with very little. Moreover, race relations, as in all Southern States, were difficult particularly during the years of Presidential Reconstruction. Low cotton prices during the first few years after the Civil War along with difficult farming seasons stalled black progress. These conditions, along with pressure from authorities of the Freedmen's Bureau in Alabama, pushed black people toward tenancy and sharecropping. The bureau forced many blacks to sign work contracts, forcing them into sharecropping and tenant farming. In return they often only received a small share of the crop according to how much of the expenses they contributed. This share was often one third or half, if the tenant contributed to the production costs. Just as concerning for the freedmen was the fact that Alabama's constitutional convention in September 1865, didn't provide any civil rights to African Americans with the exception of emancipation.

---

[3] Tuskegee University has gone through many name changes. For this chapter I will use Tuskegee Institute the name of the institution for much of the period this chapter covers

The state constitutional convention basically revived the old free African American code for all blacks.[4]

Help in Odd Places

Black people in Tuskegee wanted to be independent. However, conditions didn't make this easy. The first help for blacks in Alabama came with the end of Presidential Reconstruction and the beginning of Radical Reconstruction in 1867. Congress placed each southern state under a military governor, with the exception of Tennessee because it had ratified the Fourteenth Amendment. This amendment granted African Americans citizenship and equal protection under the law. Congress also required each southern state to construct new state constitutions granting equal rights to African Americans, including the right to vote for African American men. African Americans quickly joined and supported the Republican Party and helped shape politics in the state until the end of Alabama's reconstruction in 1874.

The return to power of the Redeemers, a group of Southern leaders who introduced the historically inaccurate "lost cause" narrative in response to the positive changes in the south during Congressional Reconstruction made life difficult for African Americans. Even before the end of Reconstruction, organizations such as the Ku Klux Klan and the Knights of the White Camelia violently dissuaded black from political activities. The fact that Tuskegee was Macon County's center of African American political resistance made it an easy target. Black political leaders in Tuskegee often held meetings at the local AME Zion church, which eventually became Butler Chapel. In June 1870, local State Senate representative James Alston participated in a political meeting at the church. After the conclusion of the meeting, white residents attacked him and his family at their home. This incident chased the State Senator out of Macon County. However, the mob was not satisfied. Hearing a rumor that Alson may have returned to the

---

[4] Bethel, Elizabeth. "The Freedmen's Bureau in Alabama." *The Journal of Southern History* 14, no. 1 (1948): 49-92. doi:10.2307/2197710.

community was hiding out in the church, local whites raided the church killing two church members.[5]

Former Slaves, Former Slave Masters, Republicans and Democrats work together

African Americans throughout Macon County desperately wanted a school that could train future educators, farmers, and tradesmen. Centered in the town of Tuskegee, the overwhelmingly majority black town had the opportunity to be a hub for all of the rural townships outside Tuskegee including Macedonia, Notasulga, and Simmons Chapel. Most of the residents of these towns in the 1880s were tenants and often moved from farm to farm. But some early leaders did emerge. Lewis Adams was born a slave around 1843. By 1880 the skilled shoemaker had established himself as a farmer and political boss of Tuskegee's black community. During that year two Democratic Party candidates for office approached him asking him for his support. Adams promised to endorse the candidates with the condition that they support a normal school for African Americans in Macon County. After their election the two politicians kept their promise and sponsored a bill in the State House creating the Normal School in Tuskegee. Adams worked closely with George Washington Campbell, an insurance broker and former slave master, to lay the groundwork for Tuskegee. Campbell and Adams contacted Samuel Chapman Armstrong to ask for suggestions for a leader of the new school. Chapman, remembering his old student, nominated Washington who became the school's first principal.[6]

Adams and Campbell's relationship with Tuskegee continued long after the creation of Tuskegee. Eventually, they spearheaded the purchase of a large plantation of about 1000 acres where the campus would reside.

---

[5] U.S. Department of the Interior & National Parks Services *Butler Chapel African Methodist Episcopal Zion Church*, NPS Form 10-900-a, OMB No. 1024-0018 (Macon County, AL, 1995).

[6] Amalia K. Amaki and Amelia Boynton Robinson, *Tuskegee* (Alabama: Arcadia Publishing, 2013), 26-7; Washington, *Up From Slavery*, 120.

Washington in his autobiography, *Up From Slavery*, expressed his gratitude to both men:

> Mr. Campbell is a merchant and banker, and had had little experience in dealing with matters pertaining to education. Mr. Adams was a mechanic, and had learned the trades of shoemaking, harnessmaking, and tinsmithing during the days of slavery. He had never been to school a day in his life, but in some way he had learned to read and write while a slave. From the first, these two men saw clearly what my plan of education was, sympathized with me, and supported me in every effort. In the days which were darkest financially for the school, Mr. Campbell was never appealed to when he was notwilling to extend all the aid in his power. I do not know two men, one an ex-slaveholder, one an ex-slave, whose advice and judgment I would feel more like following in everything which concerns the life and development of the school at Tuskegee than those of these two men.[7]

The important thing to remember is that Tuskegee Institute, and, indeed, the black community of the town of Tuskegee prospered as a result of a combination of self-determination as well as the cultivation of relationships with white men and women who were either interested or could be persuaded to assist black people. Ironically the town of Tuskegee's emergence as a major black town was created out of a deal between a former slave who was willing to deal with a political party that was not particularly seen as friendly to black people. Black people in Tuskegee leveraged their power and, because of that, gained concessions. This was an unlikely partnership similar to the one between Rahab and the people of Israel. The partnership between black leaders of Tuskegee and white political leaders was unlikely but also a major factor in the community's success.

---

[7] Washington, *Up From Slavery*, 120-121;

The University, Church, Town, and Countryside

One noticeable thing about the Tuskegee community is how long its reach was. By 1900 a well-established business community lived either on or near the campus. These older residents united with the educators and recent migrants to create a community that pushed residents toward financial and social independence. As more Blacks moved to Tuskegee, other businesses and services, in addition to the institute, came to the town including groceries, dentists, physicians, and planters. The community built the only hospital in the region for African Americans.

Religious life was an important aspect life in Tuskegee. There were a number of churches near Tuskegee, including the Mount Olive Missionary Baptist Church, which was the church that Washington and C.H. Evans, the head of the Building Construction department attended. Another important church was the Butler Chapel AME Zion. Butler Chapel was founded in 1865 by Reverend John Butler. Indeed, this church was the initial location of Tuskegee Institute. It is reported that Solomon Derry, the second pastor of Butler Chapel, was one of the first Black teachers in Tuskegee and that he had a school with more than 250 students.[8]

Religious life went further than church services. Tuskegee Institute had a Bible Training School on campus that regularly sponsored Macon and Adjacent communities Ministers' institutes. These institutes weren't just bible training sessions but they focused on helping local ministers develop a more progressive spirit. The institutes also provided a platform for Tuskegee leaders like Washington to encourage local ministers to link spiritual matters with race progress. For example, at a ministers' institute meeting in 1906, Washington encouraged ministers to "encourage our young men to go into business. The financial hope of our race rests largely on our young men going into business. The church

---

[8] "History," *Mt. Olive Missionary Baptist Church* (Tuskegee, AL) http://www.mtolivebaptistchurchtuskegee.org/history, assessed December 8, 2017.

will be better off financially. ... We must teach our people to spend their money with friends of the race."[9]

Agents for the town and countryside

One of the ways that Tuskegee Institute supported the community was by sharing its talent with the larger community, particularly the small farming settlements nearby. The leaders at Tuskegee and the local Tuskegee newspaper, *The Messenger*, worked together to promote moral and economic reforms. *The Messenger*, edited by C.J. Calloway a faculty member at Tuskegee, promoted sustainable farming and black self-determination. Calloway, like many progressives, believed that temperance and abstention from gambling should be promoted. One of his editorials stated that "parents should especially look after their sons with a view to seeing that they do not spend their time in gambling. There is no habit which will prove more harmful to the people of this county than gambling." Calloway encouraged farmers to work hard so that they could purchase land. Calloway and other leaders in Tuskegee believed that farm ownership led to more stable families and communities. Calloway, just like Washington, argued that one of the problems with tenant farming was that tenants moved too much. They believed that land owners were more likely to stay in communities than tenants who were more likely to leave. On one occasion Calloway encouraged poorer residents in Tuskegee town to move back to the countryside and rent a farm "or working on a farm for someone else."[10]

The work to establish a community of landowners extended well-beyond editorials and speeches. Calloway kept an eye out for opportunities for black people to purchase land and promoted these opportunities in his newspaper. In 1912, he organized the Home Seekers Land Company, a stock company that attempted to help African Americans acquire property. Washington also promoted Black landownership and worked diligently to make it a reality for Tuskegee

---

[9] *The Messenger*, April 20, 1906,

[10] *The Messenger*, September 14, 1906 and April 5, 1907.

residents. In 1901, with the help of white businessmen, he created the Southern Improvement Company. This company purchased four thousand acres of land not far from Tuskegee Institute. The company sold plots of land up to eighty acres at a good price with reasonable credit. Washington later formed the Tuskegee Farm and Improvement Company. The company purchased 1800 acres of land in Macon County and sold forty acre tracts to Black people. This farming community, called Baldwin Farms, was only open to Tuskegee graduates. Residents also had to be married to qualify for the program and had to pay a ten percent down payment.[11]

As an industrial school, the promotion of agriculture was a major goal of Tuskegee. George Washington Carver, was a renowned scientist and chair of the Department of Agriculture. Shortly after his arrival, Carver helped organize started organizing agricultural farmers' institutes at Tuskegee. These agricultural fairs brought local farmers to Tuskegee where they met and interacted with the members of the agricultural department at Tuskegee. Many farmers brought their families to these events, something that was encouraged by the organizers who always found opportunity to promote the importance of family and community. Carver also played an instrumental role in the Tuskegee newspaper, the *Tuskegee Messenger*. He was a regular contributor and offered his advice on a variety of farming techniques, but particularly encouraged farmers to focus on vegetable crops and the development of farms. Carver also answered questions from local farmers in the newspaper, this information often focused on how to replenish the land that was depleted by cotton production.[12]

These institutes attempted to bring information about scientific farming to the poorer residents in the rural areas surrounding Tuskegee. Although these institutes were very successful, many farmers and tenants didn't have the ability to travel to Tuskegee to benefit from these

---

[11] Robert E. Zabala and Sarah T. Warren "From Company to Community: Agricultural Community Development in Macon County, Alabama, 1881 to the New Deal," Agricultural History 72, no. 2 (1998): 460-9. http://www.jstor.org/stable/3744393

[12] *The Messenger*, March 2 and March 6, 1906;

opportunities. Responding to the need, Washington and other Tuskegee leaders took their institutes on the road. This work, called extension work, sent Tuskegee faculty and teachers from Tuskegee into the farms of Macon County. Sponsored in part by northern philanthropists initially in the early 1900s and later by the federal government, the Negro Cooperative Farm Demonstration was the first of a series of programs initiated by Tuskegee leaders to help Black farmers out of poverty. By 1906 the United States Department of Agriculture started funding the program and selected Thomas Monroe Campbell, a former Tuskegee student to work with the farmers in Macon County. Campbell tried to help farmers farm better and improve their values.[13]

Tuskegee Women

Even though they didn't hold the highest administrative positions at Tuskegee, there were a number of Black women faculty at Tuskegee. Black women also headed the Department of Domestic Service at Tuskegee Institute. Margaret Murray Washington, the wife Washington, was the Principal and Director of this department. This gave her authority over the students in this department and the responsibility to work with faculty and to develop a curriculum. Along with other female faculty members and the wives of the male faculty members, Washington formed the Tuskegee Woman's Club. This organization was the major women's organization in Tuskegee and it was formed with the idea to spread information throughout the greater Tuskegee community. They went into the jails and educated women inmates on cleanliness and motherhood. They also provided educational assistance to them. Another major avenue of work for the Women's Club was the promotion of temperance. The club also held regular mother's meetings that mentored and provided assistance to poorer women. As part of

[13] Allen W. Jones "Voices for Improving Rural Life: Alabama's Black Agricultural Press, 1890-1965," Agricultural History 58, no. 3 (1984): 212. http://www.jstor.org/stable/3743075; Karen J. Ferguson "Caught in 'No Man's Land': The Negro Cooperative Demonstration Service and the Ideology of Booker T. Washington, 1900-1918." Agricultural History 72 (winter 1998) 41.

this endeavor they sponsored night schools for everyone and Sunday School services.[14]

Black women were often at the forefront of activities in Tuskegee. Most of the teachers in the town and countryside were Black women. For example, the school sponsored the quarterly County Teacher's Institute, an institution primarily organized and run by women. This institute provided information and practicums for teachers on subjects such as principles of healthy living, the role of the teacher in the community, and teaching English in rural schools.[15]

Conclusion

Booker T. Washington's dreams of an independent black community may not have been completely realized. Indeed, his final speech in 1915 occurred right before the major urban migrations soon to occur throughout the South. Blacks would never again own as much land as they did in 1915. However, the institution he built and the Black community that congregated around that institution remain more than a century after his death. Tuskegee University remains an excellent institution of higher learning that continues to inspire the town and the surrounding community. Nonetheless, it's important to remember two things about the success of Tuskegee: (1) Black people prospered because they adopted a plan of self-determination and property ownership and (2) Black people in Tuskegee were willing to collaborate with people many may not consider likely partners. Just as the Israelites' relationship with Rahab led to their success at Jericho, African American's relationship with unlikely partners led to Tuskegee's success.

---

[14] Margaret M. Washington, "The Tuskegee Women's Club," *Southern Workman* (August 1920), 367.

[15] *The Messenger*, March 13, 1908.

FREEDMEN'S TOWN
BUILDING TOMORROW TODAY

"The people of Texas are informed that, in accordance with a proclamation from the Executive of the United States, all slaves are free. This involves an absolute equality of personal rights and rights of property between former masters and slaves, and the connection heretofore existing between them becomes that between employer and hired labor. The freedmen are advised to remain quietly at their present homes and work for wages. They are informed that they will not be allowed to collect at military posts and that they will not be supported in idleness either there or elsewhere."[1]

These words read by Major-General Gordon Granger after assuming command over the District of Texas when he arrived in Galveston, Texas, still resonate more than one hundred and fifty years later. More than two months earlier on April 9, 1865, General Robert E. Lee, the highest-ranking Confederate officer, surrendered his Army of Northern Virginia at Appomattox Court House after the fall of Richmond City, the capital of the Confederacy. Some small skirmishes occurred over the ensuring weeks, but most Confederate generals quickly surrendered. On May 12 and 13, Confederate and Union soldiers near Brownsville, Texas engaged in the Battle of Palmito Ranch, the final battle of the Civil War. More than a month later, Granger issued his order.

The day of the order, the nineteenth of June, is now recognized as Juneteenth, an African American Emancipation Day. One question

---

[1] Gordon Granger, "General Orders, no. 3, as reprinted in *New York Times*, July 7, 1865, http://www.nytimes.com/1865/07/07/news/texas-important-orders-general-granger-surrender-senator-johnson-arkansas.html.

remains: Why did it take so long for Texas slaves to learn about the Emancipation Proclamation?

Early Formation of Freedmen's Town

Abraham Lincoln issued his Emancipation Proclamation effective on January 1, 1863 even though the Confederate states in rebellion against the Union didn't recognize its authority. As the Union Army travelled throughout the south, however, they freed slaves in accordance with the Proclamation. However, in areas unoccupied by Union troops, slavemasters often didn't adhere to the Proclamation. Other masters knowing of the Proclamation and not wanting to comply, took their slaves into Texas, which was still relatively untouched by Union troops. By the time Granger arrived in Texas, approximately 250,000 slaves lived in Texas.[2]

Just like Lincoln's Proclamation, General Granger's order took some time to be fully implemented. Some masters didn't immediately tell their slaves. Others, far off plantations, didn't receive official word until later. Nonetheless, the effects of Granger's order set off a wave of events that brought increasing numbers of Blacks from the rural plantations into urban centers such as Galveston, Houston, and Dallas.

Juneteenth, as the former slaves referred to it, had tremendous ramifications for Houston. The young city already had an African American population. In 1850 and 1860 slaves comprised more than 20 percent of the city's population. Many of them, almost all formerly enslaved, lived in the area directly adjoining the city's downtown area known as the Fourth Ward. In 1841, the Methodist Church organized a church there. Included in the roughly 70 founding members were thirty-two African Americans. Ten years later, Black people had formed their own church with a White minister, as required by law. This church seems to have been very forward-thinking for the period. Not simply

---

[2] Diana Ramey Berry, In Texas, History of Slavery unique—but not brief, November 8, 2014 *MySanAntonio.com*, http://www.mysanantonio.com/opinion/commentary/article/In-Texas-history-of-slavery-unique-but-not-5879057.php)

interested in attending to the believers' spiritual needs, it also was involved in promoting social issues. In 1858, a local newspaper reported that there was a school in the African Methodist Episcopal Church.[3]

General Granger's order led to waves of African American freed people migrating to Houston and, in particular, the Fourth Ward. Invigorated by their freedom, hundreds, perhaps thousands, of former slaves moved from the rural plantations into urban environments in search of jobs, freedom, and a new life. Many of these freed people came from the vast cotton plantations along the Brazos River. They could take San Felipe Road directly to the Fourth Ward. Eventually, Black people would refer to this area as Freedmen's Town—but the names Fourth Ward and Freedmen's Town were used interchangeably. Because of the migration, the Black population grew considerably. Between 1870 and 1910, it rose from roughly 1,300 persons to 6,400.[4]

Building Relationships for Tomorrow

Tremendous obstacles awaited African Americans in Freedmen's Town. Not only did they have to think about their daily needs, they also wanted to lay a foundation for the next generation. Most new residents brought very few possessions with them. Overcrowding also was a concern for the Fourth Wardwhich lacked decent sanitation and a decent transportation system.

The small ward without any room to expand made the best of it. Because of the overall poverty, the residents constructed small, row houses. In 1870, only 27 percent of homes were occupied by single families and roughly 46 percent of the population lived with other people or families. Residents often took in boarders who may have been able to help the owner earn money to pay some expenses. Other Blacks

---

[3] Cary D. Wintz, "The Emergence of a Black Neighborhood: Houston's Fourth Ward, 1865-1915 in *Urban Texas: Politics and Development* ed. by Char Miller and Heywood T. Sanders, 96-100.

[4] Wintz, 99-100

worked and lived in the shanty towns that existed around the local hotels including the Capital Hotel, that served White clientele.[5]

During the late nineteenth and early twentieth century, the area around Walters and Preston Street, in the northern part of the Fourth Ward, just south of Buffalo Bayou was perhaps the city's poorest area. An area that floods with ease, it was a place filled with transients who had nowhere to go. The area also included a number of bars, saloons, brothels, and pool halls. One of these places was Lucretia Davis' popular saloon and restaurant. This section of the city was integrated and it included African Americans, Italians, Germans, Mexicans, and others, often living in the same homes. This was a location for the most outcast residents but an area open to all and it was one of the few places where Blacks and Whites lived in the same homes, albeit sometimes engaging in the underworld. For example, Dee Clark, a 24-year-old African American owner of a lodging house counted Goldie Bontee, a sixteen-year-old prostitute from Louisiana, as one of her residents. The same was the case for Alice Clark, a 29-year-old Black woman, who operated a lodging house that included at least one White woman.[6]

Not too far away from this section was a more affluent community located on Rusk Avenue. This area was much more residential and its population often lived there for generations. The Rose family is one example. Julia Rose, was a local seamstress who lived with her four children between 1880 and at least 1900. Rose was married to an engineer but her husband died sometime between 1880 and 1900 and she maintained the house. Her neighbor, Robert Raboin, was a fifty-year-old Black police detective who lived ,with his wife, Florence. Like the area around Buffalo Bayou, relations between races appeared

---

[5] 1900 U.S. Census, Houston Ward 4, Harris, Texas, *Roll* 1642, *Page* 19B, *Enumeration District* 0068; *FHL microfilm:* 1241642, digital image, (*http://www.ancestry.com:* assessed December 7, 2017) ; Wintz, 101.

[6] 1900 U.S. Census, Houston Ward 4, Harris, Texas, *Roll* 1642, *Page* 15B, *Enumeration District* 0068; *FHL microfilm:* 1241642, Lucretia Davis, digital image, (*http://www.ancestry.com:* assessed December 7, 2017); 1900 U.S. Census, Houston Ward 4, Harris, Texas, *Roll* 1642, *Page* 4A, *Enumeration District* 0068; *FHL microfilm:* 1241642, Dee Clark and Alice Clark, digital images, (*http://www.ancestry.com:* assessed December 7, 2017);

remarkably fluid at times. John Hammock, a White man, openly lived there with his Black wife, Louisa, and three children from at least 1880.

Over the years, the Hammocks, like many other homeowners in the area, had boarders. These boarders helped him pay the bills and worked with him at his business. Their boarders over the years included Black and White people. By 1900, Hammock's home included their daughter Lula's husband, Clarence, and their two children. Other residents on this street included preachers and hack drivers.[7]

Churches and Institutions Building for the Future

African American residents in the Fourth Ward proved effective organizers and businesspersons. As noted earlier, the African American Methodist Church, by 1880 renamed the Trinity United Methodist Church, was the first Black church in the area. Once emancipation happened, local Black residents quickly established autonomy over their church. They paid its White ownersfor the building and moved the church to a new location in Freedmen's Town. By that time, the small mission church had a group of seven Black men as trustees who were responsible for the mortgage.[8]

Antioch Missionary Baptist Church was one of the other early Black churches in the Fourth Ward. Established immediately after the Civil War, Antioch became the most influential church in Freedmen's Town and some of the city's most prominent Black leaders were members. Antioch is a particularly important example of the close relationships between White missionaries and Black Houstonians. In 1866, Antioch was established by local Blacks and White missionaries and I.S.

---

[7] 1900 U.S. Census, Houston Ward 4, Harris, Texas, *Roll* 1642, *Page* 1B, *Enumeration District* 0068, *FHL microfilm* 1241642, John Hammock, digital image, (*http://www.ancestry.com:* assessed December 7, 2017); *1880 U.S. Census, Houston, Harris, Texas* Roll *1309*; Page 149C, Enumeration District 076, Family History Film *1255309*,, John Hammock, digital image, (http://www.ancestry.com: assessed December 7, 2017.

[8] Alpha Henderson, "From Whence we Came," Trinity United Methodist Church, assessed December 7, 2017. http://www.trinityeastumc.org

Campbell became the minister. Campbell, however, soon left the church and was succeeded by John Henry "Jack" Yates.[9]

Antioch truly emerged as a prominent church in Freedmen's Town during Yates's tenure. Born a slave in Gloucester County, Virginia, Yates was living in Texas by the early 1860s. After emancipation, he came to Houston. He oversaw the construction of a new church edifice that was completed in 1879 on land owned by the church. Yates and his congregation believed that it was important for the church to pay for the land and receive the deed for the church, as it protected the church from interference from racist White authorities. Like the most progressive churches, Antioch found ways to us its members' talents. For example, Richard Allen, an architect and church trustee, designed the building.[10]

In some ways, Richard Allen was similar to Yates. He was originally born a slave in Virginia and his master moved from Virginia to Texas before the Civil War. Once freed, Allen, who didn't have formal education, gained a reputation within the city as a skilled architect, eventually designing the bridge across Buffalo Bayou (Fourth Ward) and the home of the mayor of Houston. Allen worked hard as well to build a political legacy for African Americans in Texas. He was elected to the Texas House of Representatives in 1869, the first African American in Texas to be so distinguished.

Allen remained active after the 1870s in Republican Party politics and in 1878, he ran unsuccessfully for Lieutenant Governor of Texas. By the late 1870s, at a time when the Republican Party and African Americans found themselves restricted politically, he became interested in the Kansas Exodus movement. This movement, strong throughout the south, emerged from the belief by many in the African American

---

[9] Robert A. Baker, *The Blossoming Desert—A Concise History of Texas Baptists* (Waco: Word, 1970); Rosalie Beck, "Israel S. Campbell, *Handbook of Texas Online*, accessed December 09, 2017, http://www.tshaonline.org/handbook/online/articles/fcabj.

[10] Cindy George, The Rev. John Henry Yates: A shining legacy unfettered, The Houston Chronicle, May 19, 2016, http://www.houstonchronicle.com/local/history/article/The-Rev-John-Henry-Yates-A-shining-legacy-7724485.php

community that racism was too strong in the south for them to achieve their future goals. Their solution was to advocate for African Americans to move to Kansas and to establish Black towns, so that they could provide a better life for themselves and future generations.[11]

Perhaps the greatest contribution of Black leaders was their work to establish Black institutions of higher education. In particular, Black leaders worked with two White female missionaries, Jennie Peck and Florence Dysart, to establish the Houston Baptist Academy. This academy started as an industrial school, meaning that students learned basic skills and vocational training. Eventually would become Texas Southern University. Black leaders also worked with White missionaries to establish a home school program for young children, many of whom had single mothers.[12]

Another community endeavor that promoted the community's interests was the Gregory Institute. Until 1870, Freedmen's Bureau schools existed around the entire city for African Americans. This does not mean that all African Americans had equal access to education. In 1870, the Texas Legislature established the Gregory Institute, a high school. Many Black students in the schools throughout the city were transferred to the Gregory Institute. Historians believe that Richard Allen played an instrumental role in getting the legislature to incorporate the Institute. Until the 1920s, this was the only public high school for African Americans in Houston.

The area around the Gregory Institute became a hub for the intellectual pursuits of Black Houston. Near the Institute was the Colored Carnegie

---

[11] Merline Pitrie, "Richard Allen: The Chequered Career of Houston's First Black State Legislature in eds. Howard Beeth and Cary D. Wintz in *Black Dixie: Afro-Texan History and Culture in Houston* (College Station: Texas A&M University Press, 1992.) ed. Beeth, Howard and Cary D. Wintz. " Merline Pitre, *Through Many Dangers, Toils and Snares: The Black Leadership of Texas, 1868–1900* (Austin: Eakin, 1985); *Handbook of Texas Online,* Alwyn Barr and Cary D. Wintz, "Allen, Richard," accessed December 09, 2017,http://www.tshaonline.org/handbook/online/articles/fal24.

[12] Women's Baptist Home Mission Society, *Minutes of the Baptist Home* Society Thirteenth Annual Meeting (Chicago: R.R. Donnelley and Sons), 43-44; Priscilla T. Graham, 150 Years *"Standing Strong" (Lulu: 2016),* 22

Libary which was formally opened in 1910 with assistance from E.O. Smith, the Institute's principal.[13]

Looking to the future

Although the Black community in Fourth Ward was not as financially as well off as those in Jackson Ward and Tulsa, the community did demonstrate a remarkable dedication to looking forward. In addition to having a number of masonic lodges and other similar organizations, local leaders focused their activism toward building schools and institutions that would enhance the future of the next generation. By the early twentieth century, the community also had a variety of businesses, restaurants, a movie theater, and a park for a Negro League baseball team. Much of the main social activities occurred on West Dallas Street.[14]

As the district became more established, more Black professionals moved into the area. One of the most important things that happened to the community was the development of Ancient Order of Pilgrims, a fraternal organization established in 1882 for the specific purpose of helping Blacks.

This organization, like similar ones, provided insurance and loans to its members. In 1926, the organization built a beautiful building in the Fourth Ward. This building not only housed the organization, but it also served as rental spaces for other Black businesses. This was where the Black chamber of commerce met, led in the early years by H. Spivey and O.K. Manning, one of the first secretaries. N.A. Franklin also had her beauty school in the building.[15]

---

[13] Wintz, 106

[14] Jarred Stewart, "Buffalo Stadium and Segregated Baseball," *East Texas History*, accessed December 10, 2017, http://easttexashistory.org/items/show/163; Rob Fink, *Playing in Shadows: Texas and Negro League Baseball* (Lubbock, TX: Texas Tech University Press, 2010)

[15] Priscilla Graham, *Texas Historical African American Historical Markers* (Lulu: 2016), 78.

Moving on to secure a better future

Communities decline for a variety of reasons, and one of the reasons might be voluntary. In 1910, Black doctors organized in the Fourth Ward as well and established the Union Hospital. This hospital was the only African Americans hospital in Houston until the Houston Negro Hospital opened in 1923. By the 1920s, however, residents of the Fourth Ward realized that even though their community had tremendous history, its location andresidential segregation meant that there was little room for their community to grow. Because of its location in an expanding downtown location, the Second Ward didn't have suburban property that could be purchased and subdivided to African Americans.

The Third Ward and later the Fifth, by contrast, had more area to expand. By the 1920s the Third Ward surpassed the Fourth Ward in population. A new high school for African Americans, the second in the city, was erected in the 1920s as well as a hospital. Houston's Negro Junior College, which would become Texas Southern University, was moved to the Third Ward, a decision that would ensure that the Third Ward would be the center of Black business and social community. The final breaking point for the Fourth Ward happened during World War II when, by the use of eminent domain, the city acquired roughly 38 acres of property in the ward to create San Felipe Courts. Even though the owners petitioned the act to the Supreme Court, their petition to the court was rejected. This subsided housing project was restricted to White military families completely pushing Blacks out.

Worse yet, the city erected a wall between San Felipe Courts and the remaining Black community. Other destructions occurred, the beautiful Carnegie Library that was constructed by the son-in-law of Booker T. Washington, William Pittman, was destroyed to make way for the interstate expansion.[16]

---

[16] Wintz, 106; Steven Strom, *Houston Lost and Unbuilt* (Austin: University of Texas Press, 2010), 23; Claudia Feldman, "Is it too late to save Freedmen's Town?" *Houston Chronicle*, http://www.houstonchronicle.com/news/houston-texas/houston/article/Freedmen-s-Town-dead-or-alive-6829518.php

Even though very little remains of old Freedmen's Town , its legacy remains in the bricks made to pave the streets. In the early twentieth century, without assistance from the city, local African Americans paved the streets with the bricks they had made. It is possible that former slaves who had heard Granger's orders in 1865 laid some of those bricks.

Whether this is true or not, the bricks, constructed by former slaves and their descendants, still survive today and they stand as a testament that African Americans have always believed in building tomorrow today.

Conclusion

I believe that the time has come when we as a race should begin preparing to enter upon a new policy and a new program. In plain but in emphatic words I want to suggest whether the time has not come when we should get off the defensive in things that concern our present and future, and begin to inaugurate everywhere an aggressive and constructive progressive policy in business, industry, education, moral and religious life and our conduct generally. We must follow the teachings of the Master when He said, "Overcome evil with good."—Booker T. Washington[1]

Four years ago, I wrote an opinion piece titled: "Losing Land and Agency a Troubling Trend." The piece traced the downward trend in Black land ownership. In 1915, African Americans owned appriximately 15 million acres of land. Today, we collectively own less than half that amount. Most of the communities explored in this book today follow a similar trajectory. Indeed, many of them no longer exist or are in severe decline.[2]

As a people who largely came from slavery, our churches, institutions, and businesses have historically provided a psychological boost to our community. Unfortunately, there is a strain of thought in our community today that dismisses much of our past success by viewing success stories as mere exceptions to the rule. Instead of viewing and dismissing the lives of community builders like Booker T. Washington, Maggie Lena Walker, and John Merrick, we should consider their

---

[1] Booker T. Washington, "National Negro Business League Address," (Speech, Muskogee OK, August 19, 1914), Booker T. Washington Society, http://www.btwsociety.org/library/speeches/11.php

[2] Carey H. Latimore IV, "Losing Land and Agency; A Troubling Trend." *Your Black World*, March 11, 2013, http://yourblackworld.net/2013/03/11/dr-carey-h-latimore-losing-land-and-agency-a-troubling-trend/

accomplishments as models for community renewal. Each of these African American leaders had a strong faith in God, a belief in what Black people could accomplish, and a commitment to mentoring the next generation. All of them made the choice to define their lives by faith and agency. They refused to quit even under the most difficult circumstances. These men and women did not accomplish this by viewing themselves as mere exceptions. Indeed, they saw themselves as part of the entire community.

In many ways, community leaders from older generations had a different outlook than many of our current leaders. Today, many of our leaders seem to view our community as incapable of improving without larger changes in American society. While larger structural changes in our nation are necessary, this type of thinking has stripped us of our entire being. As communities like Mound Bayou, Greenwood, and Seneca Village prove, Black people can thrive under the most difficult conditions. Therefore, it is self-defeating to think that our communities today cannot accomplish anything without external help.

Evaluating these communities also suggests the time has come to reexamine Booker T. Washington's accomplishments. Many years ago, I attended a community debate about the lives of Booker T. Washington and W.E.B. Du Bois. The young people, assisted by the elders, openly criticized Washington for his conservative political positions. In comparison, they lauded Du Bois because of his unflinching commitment to civic equality. Such a position on Washington is short-sighted. Certainly, Washington's political associations when evaluated today may look backward. If we look beyond this and toward his articulation of Black nationalism, we can clearly see his desire to create a Black nation. While he certainly expected integration to happen one day, he also expected Black people to set up and controlled their own economic, social, and religious institutions. His influence in helping African Americans by documenting and cultivating Black communities is almost forgotten today. Washington's vision inspired many Black leaders to establish industrial schools of instruction and to promote a strict code of morality and uplift. African Americans could take pride in their Black stores, universities, and churches. I am certain that Booker T. Washington and others did not see integration as something that would lead to the destruction of this foundation. Their vision of American integration did not mean complete assimilation.

Toward the end of his life, there are hints of an emerging radicalism in Washington's thought. In the excerpt above, Washington asks Black people to adopt an "aggressive and constructive policy" in all matters. What Washington was asking Black people to do was to plot and construct their destinies. Indeed, celebrating Washington's impact does not mean that we should denigrate Du Bois. Both ideologies work well when put together. We should seek civil rights and equality without ceasing. At the same time, we will never accomplish that goal without a strong economic and spiritual foundation.

The men and women in the historic communities of this book did just that. They pressed forward in a world while enduring extreme racism and oppression. Even under those circumstances, Black people often left their homes sometimes travelling thousands of miles to pursue their desired destinies. For example, the African American community at Mound Bayou had its genesis in the relationships between Black people at Davis Bend. Even when they moved, they maintained their connection to their church and community. They did this because they recognized the church, the schoolhouse, and the Black business all represented the needs of the community.

Today, many of the institutions that have elevated our community in the past are at a crossroads. Demographic changes have required our institutions to be more flexible. Moreover, as a result of integration, African Americans have many more choices about where to spend their time. How our institutions can remain culturally relevant in an integrated America is perhaps one of most vexing questions for our current generation. We must ask the question, "Does integration mean that there are no benefits to maintaining our own institutions?"

I believe that African Americans can thrive in an integrated world. To do so, we must maintain the cultural and institutional value of the institutions that have historically been at our foundation. W.E.B. Du Bois wrote more than 100 years ago:

> "the history of the American Negro is the history of this strife,--this longing to attain self-conscious manhood, to merge his double self into a better and truer self. In this merging he wishes neither of the older selves to be lost. He would not Africanize America, for America has too much to teach the world and Africa. He would not bleach his Negro soul in a flood of white Americanism, for he knows that Negro blood has a message for the world. He simply wishes to make it possible for a man to be both a Negro and an American, without being cursed and spit upon by his fellows, without having the doors of Opportunity closed roughly in his face."[3]

Du Bois understood that African Americans have a "twoness" to their existence—being black and American. This means that African Americans will always have some fundamental need for affirmation that American institutions will never be able to offer; our own institutions must provide that. At the same time, the impact of American institutions can augment the reaching of African Americans' full potential.

We must take an active role in immersing ourselves in our history. A foundational knowledge of our history provides perspective and purpose to life. I think this is what Booker T. Washington referred to when he said, "Success is not to be measured by the position someone has reached in life, but the obstacles he has overcome while trying to succeed." Understanding the Black experience helps us to put the stories of our communities into a clearer perspective. Indeed, the stories in this book have not focused on comparing them to other communities, but they have evaluated how the people in those communities overcame preexisting obstacles to build them.[4]

No evaluation of the Black community is complete without discussing the role of Black church. As one can see in these chapters, the church

---

[3] W.E.B. Du Bois and Brent Hayes Edwards (editor), The Souls of Black Folk (New York: Oxford University Press, 2007), 9.

[4] Booker T. Washington, *Up From Slavery* (New York: Cosimo Inc., 2007 reprint), 19.

has been and remains the most important institution in our community. Initially, it was the center of political and social organization for the community. It provided Black people with social and economic capital, something important for success in any society. Today, that foundation shows some signs of erosion because many of our historic churches are in decline. History proves to us that communities die when residents allow their institutions to suffer. In the past, we have placed significant attention to external forces threatening our communities. Now the time has come to look inward, making changes only we can make.

To accomplish these goals, we will need to be more proactive in protecting our community landmarks. Eatonville provides a model because it is but one example of a community that views itself as a steward of its legacy. Indeed, today Eatonville is experiencing a revival. However, we need to become better stewards of the blessings that God has bestowed on us. Other communities in this study have seen a decline in Black land ownership not only through eminent domain and the construction of interstates and roads, but also because of unclear lines of ownership. In other words, our ancestors did not leave wills behind. This is but one of the easier things that we can do to help protect our resources.

I hope that now, after reading these narratives, you are as optimistic as I am about the future of our community. God has provided our community with a roadmap to success. Indeed, building the Kingdom is a spiritual quest. As Christians, we should recognize the transcendent power faith has in our lives. I hope that you will be able to continue these journeys with the faith and desire neededto rebuild, renew, and refresh our communities and institutions.